THE
CACTI
HANDBOOK

THE CACTI HANDBOOK

JOHN ELLIS

© 2007 D&S Books Ltd

D&S Books Ltd
Kerswell,
Parkham Ash, Bideford
Devon, England
EX39 5PR

e-mail us at:-
enquiries@dsbooks.fsnet.co.uk

This edition printed 2007

Distributed in the UK by SILVERDALE BOOKS
An imprint of Bookmart Ltd
Registered number 2372865
Trading as Bookmart Ltd
Blaby Road
Wigston
Leicester LE18 4SE

All rights reserved.
This book is protected by copyright. No part of it may be reproduced, stored in a retrieval system, or transmitted in any form or by any means, without the prior permission in writing of the Publisher, nor be circulated in any form of binding or cover other than that in which it is published and without a similar condition including this condition being imposed on the subsequent Publisher

ISBN 13 – 978-1-903327-63-0

Book Code: DS0186. The Cacti Handbook

Material from this book previously appeared in *Beginner's Guide to Cacti & Other Succulents.*

Creative Director: Sarah King
Designer: Debbie Fisher & Co

Fonts: TFAlambic

Printed in Thailand

1 3 5 7 9 10 8 6 4 2

Contents

Introduction	7
Part one: All about cacti & succulents	10
– What are cacti & succulents	12
– Taxonomy – the naming of plants	14
– Cacti & succulents in habitat	18
– Cultivation	22
– Propagation	36
– Problems	44
– Increasing the size of your collection	54
Part two: Cactus directory	57
Part three: Other succulents	182
Glossary	232
Index	238
Credits and bibliography	240

introduction

Introduction

I am often asked, 'Why do people grow cacti and other succulents?' Although there are many different reasons the basic answer is that, within the range of species and features of cacti and succulents, there is something to attract almost everyone with an interest in gardening and nature – as well as those who are drawn by the unusual.

Perhaps the fascination lies in their unique evolution and in the many ingenious ways in which these plants have adapted to surviving in harsh desert environments. Their methods of conserving water and their different forms of camouflage add to the attraction.

Some people grow cacti and succulents for their unusual, and sometimes even bizarre, appearance.

the cacti handbook

Even when not in flower, these plants display an amazing variety of eye-catching shapes, sizes, patterns and colours. Their flowers range from tiny to enormous (some can be several times the size of the plant). They can be dainty, pretty, stunningly audacious or, sometimes, just weird. The often-repeated myth that cacti only flower once every seven, 20 or 100 years is just that — a myth. Once a cactus or succulent has reached maturity and flowered, provided it is kept healthy and given the same favourable conditions that induced flowering in the first place, it should flower every year thereafter.

The object of this book is to help a beginner, new to the hobby, to get started. Part one explains the basics of cultivation, what makes a plant succulent, what a cactus is and how plants are named. The latter is a very controversial subject and you should read the section on taxonomy (see p. 14) for more information about the naming of plants in general, as well as for specific information about the selection of the names used within this book. To aid the understanding of someone new to growing these plants, some subjects have been simplified. If you do not understand a technical term, refer to the glossary (see p.232). Parts two and three provide a photographic introduction to some plants that a new grower may wish to consider when enlarging his or her collection.

More experienced growers will want to add more technical and comprehensive books to their library. This book is not intended to

introduction

compete with the huge – and expensive – works of the likes of Edward Anderson or Lyman Benson. You will move on to these specialist works if your interest in the hobby continues to develop. As a beginner you need a basic guide, with easy-to-follow advice, minimal use of botanical terminology, and plenty of photographs to help with the selection of plants.

BELOW: Epiphyllums are good examples of plants grown solely for the beauty of their stunning flowers.

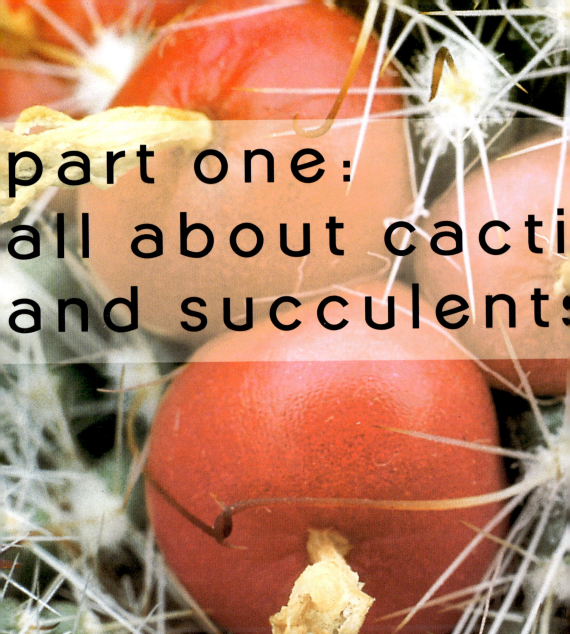

part one:
all about cacti
and succulents

What are cacti and succulents?

The definition of succulent is 'sappy, juicy, fleshy'. That is usually taken to mean a plant that has evolved the capacity for water retention. This gives it the ability to withstand periods of drought. The water retention is normally accomplished by one or more of the following:

- thickened leaves, visibly fleshy, often permanent (rather than deciduous)
- enlarged stems and/or branches
- enlarged roots or tubers

Succulents, therefore, are defined by this physical characteristic, rather than by membership of any particular family of plants. Indeed, many plant families contain both succulent and non-succulent members.

The family Cactaceae, which gives its name to cactus plants, is the principal exclusively succulent family. Although

LEFT: Pachypodium densiflorum – showing its succulent stem.

all about cacti and succulents

botanically there is no reason to do so, members of the large and distinctive cactus family are often separated from the succulent plants of other families – hence the common expression 'cacti and succulents'. Strictly speaking, this makes no sense, as cacti are succulents. Instead one should refer to 'succulents, including cacti', or, if segregation is required, 'cacti and other succulents'.

So, other than being a member of the Cactaceae, what is a cactus? Several characteristic features are used to describe a cactus, but only one need be applied for recognition purposes. Cacti have 'spine cushions', more properly called areoles. They are the oval-shaped places, often woolly, from where spines or spine remnants grow. Note that it is the spine cushions, not the spines themselves, which form the defining criterion. Not all cacti have spines, but those with few or no spines still retain the areole from where spines would have grown on their ancestors. Some plants have evolved to look very similar to cacti, such as some euphorbias. These have spines but they do not have areoles – and so they are not cacti.

ABOVE: Haworthia species, such as this H. nigra, are 'leaf succulents'. They are also examples of plants grown for their beauty when not in flower.

Taxonomy: the naming of plants

The naming of plants is one of the most controversial subjects associated with the cultivation of cacti and succulents. There is a conflict between botanists, who strive to give plants scientifically correct names, and growers, who simply want a universally used name for each plant that they grow. The problem is twofold. Firstly, the correct name for a plant cannot readily be proven, and so different taxonomists propose different names, some of which become accepted, while others are eventually rejected. Secondly, what constitutes 'a different plant'? Field studies show that, due to natural evolution over time and geographic

all about cacti and succulents

distance, significant variations may be found in plants originating from a common ancestor.

Consider a hypothetical example. A species of white-flowered cactus has been given the name 'albiflora'. Some distance away another plant – also white-flowered, but with very long spines – of the same genus has been independently named 'longispina'. Some time later, a third plant – still white-flowered, but with medium-length spines – is named 'intermedius'. Eventually botanists realise that all three are forms of the same plant. They also discover that there are many other forms with a whole range of different spine lengths, making it impossible to tell where one species (or subspecies or variety) ends and the next begins. All the plants now revert to the oldest name 'albiflora'. This is scientifically correct, but it does not suit the grower who wants to buy a plant of a particular appearance (say the long-spined form). If he is buying the plant without seeing it – by mail order perhaps – he could acquire any one of the many different forms of the plant bearing that same name.

ABOVE: Opuntia leptocaulis is often called the Desert Christmas Cactus in parts of the United States, but it is not the plant Europeans call Christmas Cactus.

LEFT: The white, slightly woolly, areoles – or spine cushions – form a spiral pattern on the rebutia species.

the cacti handbook

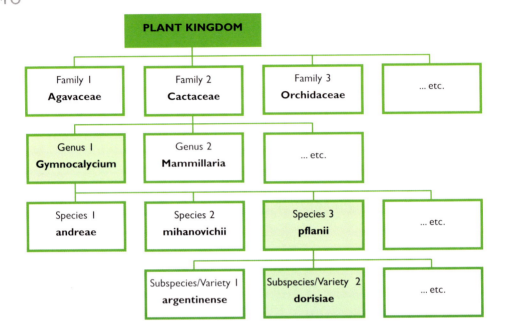

This tendency for scientific names to change as new research is undertaken means that the same species can often be seen for sale under different names. As a result, an unwary grower could buy several different labels, each accompanied by identical plants!

Theoretically, one solution to the problem would be for scientists to use scientific names and amateur growers to use 'common' names. Ideally, the common name would remain unique to a particular form of a species, while its scientific name could be changed to suit current nomenclature. Sadly, in practice, this will not work. Different common names are often applied to the same plant. For example, 'Golden Barrel' and 'Mother-in-law's Armchair' both refer to Echinocactus grusonii. In addition, completely different plants can have the same common name. 'Christmas Cactus' can refer to Opuntia leptocaulis in North America, yet it is used for schlumbergera species in Europe. The other problem with common names is language. For a naming system to be universal the same language must be used by everyone, hence the use of Latin for scientific names.

There is no easy answer to the naming problem. This book uses the scientific naming convention of Latin binomials. However, because the book is intended primarily as an aid for newcomers to the hobby, the names used are those most likely to be seen on the labels of plants offered for sale and are not necessarily those favoured by the most current taxonomy.

Latin binomials date back to the mid-1700s and were developed by the Swedish naturalist Carl Linnaeus. Their use is governed by 'The International Code of Botanical Nomenclature'. However, all a beginner needs to know is how the name is constructed. The basic principle is based on a 'family tree' of all plants. Each plant family is split into a number of genera, and each genus is split into a number of species. These in turn may be further subdivided into subspecies (designated by 'ssp.'), varieties ('var.' or 'v.') or forms ('f.' or 'fa.').

the cacti handbook

Cacti and Succulents in habitat

Succulents can be found throughout most of the world, including some alpine areas that experience very low temperatures, but most are found in the more tropical zones. With the exception of a very small number of rainforest plants, cacti come exclusively from the Americas, where their habitat extends from Canada to Patagonia and from the high Andes down to the equatorial coastlines. Although usually considered to be desert plants, it is a popular misconception that cacti and succulents can survive in truly dry deserts such as the Sahara in Africa or the Atacama in South America – some cacti do encroach here, but only where they can acquire moisture from coastal fogs. Only annuals whose seeds can lie dormant for years are able to survive without any water for very prolonged periods.

The majority of cacti and other succulents come from arid, semi-desert habitats where water is scarce but regular. Typically, these areas receive infrequent but heavy annual rains.

all about cacti and succulents

Although many growers are not fortunate enough to be able to travel to see the plants in habitat, it is worth learning a little about the conditions in which the plants grow naturally. This knowledge will aid your understanding of the conditions the plants need if they are to thrive in cultivation.

RIGHT: Arid semi-desert is a typical habitat for cacti, which grow among other plants and shrubs.

For example, plants from the high Andes (e.g. rebutia species) will be tolerant of low temperatures, but need good light as they are exposed to high light intensity and ultra-violet rays in habitat. Conversely, cacti from the Brazilian coastal regions (e.g. melocactus species) and succulents from Madagascar (e.g. some pachypodium species) cannot tolerate low temperatures and must be given artificial heat in the winter months. Rainforest plants (e.g. epiphytic cacti) do not require such pronounced 'seasons', preferring water 'a little but often' and warm, shady conditions.

AOVE: Mammillaria grahamii – cacti in habitat often seek shade under bushes or rocks.

all about cacti and succulents

Obviously it is not possible, or necessary, to recreate every plant's own natural habitat. Most cacti and succulents are perfectly happy with a typical 'semi-desert' environment, comprising a warm, sunny summer, during which they receive plenty of water at well-spaced intervals, and a cool dry winter rest. Only a minority of plants need to be treated significantly differently, but it is still worth understanding the plant's preferences – one side of a greenhouse will always be sunnier than the other, so plants should be arranged to make the best of these conditions.

the cacti handbook

Cultivation

This guide to cultivation cannot possibly cover the optimum growing conditions for all succulent plants; instead it aims to provide a suitable approach for the majority of species. Deviations from these typical conditions (e.g. the need for higher winter temperatures) are highlighted by the four symbols – relating to light, winter temperature, compost and watering – that accompany the pictures in Part two. A key to the meanings of the symbols is provided on page 60. Similarly, where particular plants need special treatment, this is described in the associated text.

all about cacti and succulents

Different people give their plants different growing conditions; the only right approach is the one that you find keeps your plants healthy. If that is different from someone else's it does not matter — do not be afraid to experiment and learn.

Where to Grow Your Plants

Where you live — the climate, available space, etc. — and what you can afford will determine where you can grow your plants. The following are some common locations and their relative merits.

Outdoor — Although a few species of succulent will survive in most places, unless you are fortunate enough to live in a frost-free country the choice of plants that can be grown in the ground outdoors is very limited. An alternative approach is to grow plants in pots on, say, a patio, and then move them to a protected location during the winter months. Many plants would benefit from such a regime.

Greenhouse — Greenhouses are generally considered to provide the best growing conditions in most of the colder countries. They offer a sheltered environment while still providing good light. Depending upon the species being grown, they may or may not need to be heated. In very hot countries open-sided 'shade houses' can provide shelter from the hot sun and from tropical rainstorms. As well as the more usual

LEFT: An outdoor collection of cacti on the island of Gran Canaria.

growing of plants in pots on greenhouse staging, some very impressive displays can be made in a larger greenhouse by planting them in raised beds. The free root room this gives them can result in impressive growth, but be warned – do not plant opuntias or large growing agaves in such beds; they will grow so quickly that they will rapidly become a problem!

Cold frame – Cold frames are relatively inexpensive and can provide excellent growing conditions for plants that need protection, but do not require extra heat. However, the size of plants that can be grown is limited and they are less convenient than a walk-in greenhouse.

Conservatory – Conservatories can give ideal growing conditions to many plants (e.g. hoyas), especially if they

ABOVE RIGHT: Growers in most countries prefer to use greenhouses to house their collections.

LEFT: Plants grow well when they get established in a raised bed within a greenhouse.

are kept frost-free in the winter months. As conservatories are also rooms for living in, they cannot provide space for as many plants as a greenhouse of the same size, but they allow more people to see your collection.

Windowsill – Many a large collection was first started on a windowsill. Provided the window faces in a direction that gives suitable light and that adequate ventilation is given to prevent scorching of the plants, many will grow quite happily on a windowsill. Obviously the size of the plants grown will be limited. Also they will tend to favour the side receiving most light, producing single-sided shows of flowers.

Under lights – The use of special horticultural lights (ordinary electric light is not suitable) can be useful in providing controlled conditions for seed raising, or to enable plants to be grown in, for example, a cellar, if no alternative location is available. However they are expensive to buy and run and so do not really provide a viable option for beginners.

Watering

Watering is the key to success or failure. Far more cacti and other succulents are killed by over-watering than by any other means. On the other hand, these plants are living things and, contrary to some people's belief, even the hardiest of desert plants cannot survive indefinitely without any water at all. During their growing period most of these plants can take plenty of water, but they must not be left standing in any surplus, and they must not be watered again until the compost has completely dried out from the previous application. The timescale for this depends upon various factors – ambient temperature, compost composition, pot type (clay pots dry out far quicker than plastic ones), etc. – but typically would be every couple of weeks in the summer months and less in the spring and autumn.

To avoid the risk of water remaining on the plants and causing damage, watering is best done either directly onto the compost around the plants or from beneath. Plunging pots into water – or flooding the trays the pots are standing in – for a few minutes is quite acceptable, providing the surplus is drained away.

With the exception of the rainforest epiphytes, plants should be given a rest period each year. A few plants (typically some of the South African Mesembs) grow during the winter months, but most cacti and other succulents are summer growers and benefit from a completely dry, cool winter rest. This rest period often promotes flowering the following spring. It is the lack of a rest that is often to blame for cacti grown in centrally heated living rooms, and watered all year round, failing to flower. The frequency of watering should be reduced gradually as winter approaches and, more importantly, gradually increased in the spring. Many cacti and other succulents grow best in acidic compost. Tap water tends to be alkaline and, over time, can gradually cause the pH to rise, inhibiting plant growth. To compensate for this some growers occasionally use chemicals (proprietary acidic fertilisers or hydrangea colorant) to acidify the water. Care should be taken as the improved water take-up can cause some plants to split. Acidified water should not be used for plants that prefer calcareous composts.

BELOW: Rebutia hoffmannii – good light and a cold, dry winter rest helps promote flower production.

the cacti handbook

Temperature

High temperatures during the growing season should not normally present a problem, provided adequate air movement is given to prevent plants from scorching and the frequency of watering is increased accordingly. Although often beneficial to flowering, low temperatures in the winter months can be damaging, or even fatal, to some plants. Consequently, though many plants are actually frost hardy in their natural environment, most growers prefer to keep their greenhouses frost-free – a minimum of approximately 5°C (40°F) – for safety. A small, enclosed area within the greenhouse may be used to maintain a higher temperature for those few species that need even more protection. The most important thing is to ensure that any plants

all about cacti and succulents

exposed to low temperatures are completely dry – the combination of cold with wet compost is often fatal. Beware of heaters that burn fossil fuels (e.g. paraffin or gas), as they give off large amounts of water as a combustion by-product, resulting in high humidity. Good air movement will help protect plants from pockets of cold and/or damp air.

The use of insulation, such as bubble glazing, will cut down on draughts and heat loss and so reduce heating bills. It will also help stop any leaks or condensation drips from the roof falling onto plants, and in summer it reduces the risk of scorching. Unfortunately, it also reduces the light intensity passing through.

LEFT: Mammillaria species – plants grown in good light have better spination. Close examination will reveal natural patterns and beauty which might otherwise be overlooked.

the cacti handbook

Light

Good light is essential for healthy plants. It must be bright enough to prevent the plants etiolating (growing tall, thin and pale), yet not so intense or close to glass that the plants scorch. Scorching can be avoided by the provision of more ventilation and/or airflow, or even some shading. Better ventilation /airflow is preferable, because shading will reduce the amount of UV light the plants receive, which will result in weaker spination on cacti, as well as later and/or less prolific flowering. One-sided light (such as on a windowsill) is not disastrous, but it will affect the growth of the plants.

Compost

Much has been written over the years about the best ingredients to be added to compost and many growers will have their own favourite recipe. In reality, however, the main criterion is that it must be free draining. Ideally it should also include some fertiliser and trace elements. The easiest way to achieve this is to take a standard houseplant potting compost and add 50% extra grit. This basic mixture can then be supplemented by the addition of yet more grit for the most water-intolerant species and/or by the addition of limestone chippings for those – particularly Mexican – plants that prefer calcareous compost. The purchase of special proprietary cactus compost is not recommended, as it can be expensive and, despite its claims to the contrary, is often insufficiently open to aid good drainage. Some growers prefer to use pure grit. This requires more frequent watering and the regular application of fertiliser.

It is common practice to 'top-dress' plants by applying a layer of grit on the surface of the compost. Apart from its decorative qualities this also helps keep the body of the plant separated from the moisture in the compost and may help deter pests from entering the soil.

LEFT: Correctly potted plants have sufficient room for growth without having too great a volume of moisture-retaining compost.

Repotting

Apart from moving plants into larger pots as they grow, repotting into fresh compost helps keep plants nourished and healthy. Ideally, small plants should be repotted annually and larger ones every two or three years. However, this is not always easy to achieve, particularly in large collections of hundreds of plants.

Never use too large a pot. Large volumes of compost will take longer to dry out and increase the risk of root loss and rot. Small pots for cacti should be chosen to give about 1–2 cm (1/2–3/4 in) around the base of the plant. This amount should be increased in proportion for larger plants. Many cacti and other succulents have shallow root systems, and for these, the use of half-pots or pans is preferable. Obviously, if a plant has a particularly large root system, then a larger pot must be provided to accommodate it.

Most growers nowadays use plastic pots, which are cheaper and more durable than clay. The latter have some advantages, however: their increased weight will help prevent tall plants from becoming top heavy; their insulating properties offer the roots more protection, and – if unglazed – they allow the compost to dry out quicker than plastic pots. Many people ask how cacti can be safely handled while repotting. Certainly care is needed and this works both ways – the spines can be painful, but also the plants themselves can be easily damaged,

all about cacti and succulents

particularly if spine clusters become entangled in gloves. A better method is to wrap layers of newspaper or pieces of polystyrene around the plant.

The ideal solution is to minimise contact with the spines. Squeeze the pot to loosen it, tip the plant on its side and shake/slide the pot off the root-ball. Once the pot is removed, the plant can be safely handled, since it does not have spines below soil level. Various home-made tools like spoons and loops of coat-hanger wire can be used to manoeuvre the plant into its new pot. Particularly tall or heavy cacti need different treatment. Use garden canes, or planks of wood, as splints. These will enable you to lay down tall plants, without the danger of snapping them. Bubble wrap is a useful way of avoiding injury

RIGHT: Two sulcorebutia species, one with tuberous roots, the other with a fibrous root system.

from/to spines. A piece of carpet can help prevent the weight of a large, heavily spined plant (such as Echinocactus grusonii) from impaling your skin. The most difficult to handle are opuntias because their glochids detach from the plant, entering and irritating the skin. A good way of handling these flat-padded plants is to put a thin piece of polystyrene packing on each side. Squeeze them gently together to grip the plant and then discard the glochid-laden material.

If the plant has been pot-bound and the root-ball is a solid mass of roots taking the shape of the old pot, it is advisable to gently and carefully loosen the roots before putting the plant into new pot.

Repotting provides the ideal opportunity to check on the health of a plant's root system and to look for pests living beneath the soil. After removing the plant, always examine the inside of the empty pot for the tell-tale white deposits left by root mealy bug.

Do not water plants for at least a week after repotting. This will give any root damage time to heal over, minimising the risk of infection and rot.

Fertiliser

The strength and frequency of fertiliser application depends upon the specific growing regime. Plants that are grown in rich compost and regularly repotted will require a less frequent application than those grown in pure grit. The latter will benefit from a dilute application at every watering. It is important not to give succulent plants too much nitrogen; they come from harsh environments where most grow slowly. Excessive amounts of nitrogen will often result in a weak, flabby plant that will be prone to disease. A potash-rich fertiliser (tomato food or similar) applied monthly during the growing season is often recommended.

BELOW: Some plants, such as Mammillaria carmenae, have soft spines and are safe to handle; others need more care!

Propagation

Sooner or later every grower will want to propagate additional plants. For most species this is not too difficult and many can be propagated either from seed or by means of cuttings.

Seed Raising

Raising plants from seed provides a cheap and rewarding means of propagation. For many species it is not difficult and, while some species are very slow and will take many years to reach maturity, most will reach flowering size in just a few years. Experiment with the easier ones, such as mammillaria, gymnocalycium or rebutia, first. The latter will often provide an encouraging show of flowers from small plants still in seed trays after only 18 months.

Seed can be obtained from a variety of sources, including garden centres, mail order specialists and collecting your own from plants that have flowered in your collection. (These seeds may well produce hybrid plants, but provide a free source of seed to practise with). Be aware that seed offered for sale may not be fresh and, although in some species the seed matures over time, in most – particularly the Stapeliads – its viability decreases with age.

all about cacti and succulents

Seeds should be sprinkled onto the surface of small pots of damp compost. With the exception of very large seeds, which can be easily handled with tweezers and pushed gently just below the surface, they should not be buried as they require light to germinate. Even new compost can contain pests, so sterilisation prior to use is strongly recommended. This can be easily achieved in a microwave oven. The seed pots must not be allowed to dry out until germination has taken place, or for the first few months afterwards. One popular way of

BELOW: Seed raising is a cheap and rewarding way of acquiring plants.

achieving this is to seal the entire pot inside a plastic bag, thus trapping the moisture, which forms as condensation and is recycled. If this method is used, sterilisation of all the materials is critical to prevent fungal growth in the humid atmosphere. An alternative is to allow good air circulation over the pots while standing them in a tray and giving them water from below. There is no correct approach: experiment and see what proves successful under your specific conditions.

Germination is usually the easy bit and should take place somewhere between a few days and a few weeks, depending upon the species being grown. This period may be accelerated by the application of

bottom heat, particularly if a timer is used to give warm days and cooler – but not cold – nights. The exception is some of the mesembryanthemums – germination of conophytum and lithops species actually appears to be inhibited by the application of heat. Once germinated, the seedlings must be carefully 'grown on' for the first year of their lives. Often getting them through their first winter is the greatest challenge; most are too small to have much in the way of reserves and so they need to be kept growing continuously. They are also susceptible to light intensity. However, with vigilance, this should not be a problem as they do give a visual indication of their health. Newly germinated seedlings will be a yellowish-green colour, but this should change after a few days to a healthy green. If they remain yellow, they are getting insufficient light and will become elongated and weak. If they turn pink, they are getting too much light and their growth will slow or stop altogether. If this happens, additional shade must be provided.

If the seedlings are not being grown using the 'plastic bag' method, two potentially fatal problems must be watched out for. The most devastating is the larvae of sciarid flies (also known as fungus gnats). These tiny worm-like creatures can devour an entire pot of seedlings in just a week or two. The sure-fire sign that they are present is the sight of tiny adult flies circling over the pots. The other problem can be the build

LEFT: Mammillaria oteroi – harvest your own seed to experiment with seed-raising techniques, but remember the resultant seedlings may be hybrids.

up of algae on the surface of the compost. This can overwhelm the smaller, slower-growing seedlings. The application of very fine grit around established seedlings will help to inhibit the growth of algae. Once they are big enough to be handled, the seedlings can be very carefully transplanted into rows in seed trays (be sure to avoid damage to the tender roots), where they can be grown on until they are large enough to plant into individual pots. The initial transplanting may be in a matter of months, or a year or more, after sowing, depending upon the species being grown and the rate of growth achieved.

BELOW: Cuttings rooting on a gritty compost, heated gently from below.

Cuttings

If the intention is to produce more plants from one already in your possession, then cuttings are usually the best way of achieving this. A few succulents are reluctant to be propagated in this way, but they are in the minority. The ideal time to take cuttings is in late spring when the plants have come into full, vigorous growth and when they have the rest of the growing season to get established.

The basic technique for both cacti and other succulents is as follows. Select a plant that has suitable side shoots or branches (i.e. large enough to be self-sustaining until the new roots form, and not too woody). Sever the cutting from the parent plant using a very sharp, sterile blade. Always ensure this is done by means of a single, clean cut. Any tearing or partial incisions will provide a starting point for fungal attack and there is a greater risk of losing the plant. Do not use scissors or secateurs, as they tend to bruise and crush the plant. If you need to cut off the woody branches of a taller cereoid cactus, you will need to use a hacksaw, or something similar, but the cut must still be made as cleanly as possible.

A few succulents will 'bleed' from the cut surfaces. Spraying them with water will usually stop this. However, do not leave the surfaces too wet, as this encourages rot.

the cacti handbook

> **WARNING:** Some succulents, particularly euphorbias, contain a sap that can be toxic and/or a skin irritant. Always take precautions to protect your eyes and wash any splashes off your skin.

The two cut surfaces (cutting and parent plant) should be dusted with a fungicide powder and left in a dry place to callous over. In the case of large cactus cuttings, this may take days, or even weeks. Only when the cut surface has healed should the cutting be stood on top of — not buried in — a suitable rooting medium. A very open, gritty compost is usually recommended, though good results have been achieved on Perlite or similar material. Place the plant in a shady location and spray it occasionally until roots begin to form — the application of bottom heat may speed up this process. Once it has rooted, treat the cutting as a mature plant.

A few of the other succulents (e.g. gasterias and adromiscus) can be propagated from leaf cuttings. Simply remove a few leaves and press them gently onto the surface of the compost. Treat them as ordinary cuttings; eventually roots and then plantlets will form and grow.

Offsets

People often ask whether the offsets that form on globular cacti (e.g. rebutia or echinopsis species) should be left in place or removed. There is no right or wrong answer to this question. Many cacti form clumps

all about cacti and succulents

naturally in habitat by offsetting, though this process can sometimes be exaggerated in cultivation. Leaving the offsets in place can result in the formation of beautiful clumps and is often the best course of action. However, if the clump becomes too large, damaged and/or unsightly, or if propagation is required, offsets can be removed by means of a sharp, sterile blade. The offsets should be treated as cuttings.

Grafting

Another technique, which is often included in books and demonstrated on television programmes, is grafting. It involves the use of a strong, growing stock plant onto which is grafted a weaker and/or slower growing plant. This is a valuable technique that can be used to speed up the growth of extremely slow plants, enable the survival of plants without chlorophyll, which could not survive alone, aid mass production of plants for the nursery trade, or salvage pieces of damaged plants. Although it is fun to experiment with, the technique cannot be considered a basic necessity and so is not described further here.

RIGHT: Gymnocalycium cultivars – virtually chlorophyll-free these plants need to be grafted to enable them to survive.

Problems

Although it may be a false alarm, always investigate a plant that looks unhappy – one that seems to be shrinking, looks soft or has lost its healthy sheen during the growing season. Prompt investigation may save the plant, or part of it, from loss and may prevent the problem from becoming more extensive and affecting other plants.

Pests

Virtually all plants attract pests and cacti and other succulents are no exception. Prevention is better than cure and the best way to avoid problems is to try to prevent pests from getting into your collection. A strict two or three week's quarantine of new acquisitions can significantly reduce the risk of infestation. All new plants should be repotted into fresh compost and examined closely for any signs of pests – both above and below the soil. It is good practice to adopt a routine of applying insecticides to new plants even if they appear to be clean. Occasional application of insecticide to your entire collection can also be a wise precaution. Certainly any infested plants discovered in a collection should be immediately removed and treated. Adjacent plants should also be treated as a further precaution. Delay between discovery and treatment will almost certainly result in the pests spreading throughout the entire collection.

Be careful when selecting an insecticide to make sure it targets the pests you are trying to eradicate and that is suitable for the plants you are applying it to. Some plants, particularly succulents such as echeverias, are very sensitive to certain chemicals. Avoid using the ready-mixed, soap-based insecticides as these are suspected of causing long-term damage to the bodies of cacti.

Left: Inspect plants regularly and take action at the first sign of trouble to keep your plants in good health.

the cacti handbook

Some of the more common pests are:

Mealy bugs – by far the most common insect to infest succulent collections, mealy bugs are small, pale, oval-shaped creatures up to about 0.5 cm (0.2 in) long. They have a white, waxy covering, which protects them from water-based insecticides, and they leave fluffy, white deposits on the plants. They can be controlled biologically by means of predatory insects but this will not completely eradicate the

ABOVE: Mealy bugs are probably the most common pests found on succulent plants.

pests. A commonly used method of killing them is to touch each individually with the tip of a fine paintbrush dipped in methylated spirits. However, this is laborious and unlikely to eradicate them completely.

Root mealy bugs – a similar, slightly smaller, but perhaps more damaging pest than mealy bugs, root mealy bugs attack the plants below soil level and so can invade a collection without being seen. They damage the root systems and so weaken plants, as well as increasing the risk of rot getting into the roots. When repotting a plant, always examine the inside of the old pot for the white deposits that indicate the presence of this pest. If found, it is advisable to wash off as much as possible of the old soil and to soak the plant in a suitable insecticide before replanting it in its new pot.

Sciarid flies – more commonly known as fungus gnats or mushroom flies, these tiny flies can be seen circling around infected plants. The flies themselves do no harm, but their larvae – which look like small, semi-transparent worms with black heads – can devour a whole pot of tender seedlings in a very short time. They can also attack mature plants and may even kill them. They thrive in damp composts, particularly those containing high proportions of peat or other humus material.

Red spider mites – despite their name these are not spiders. They are very tiny mites, barely visible to the naked eye, which cover plants with fine webbing and result in a brown scarring, particularly around the growing points of cacti. They thrive in warm, dry atmospheres, making cactus greenhouses a prime habitat for them.

Scale insects – these small, rounded pests clamp themselves firmly onto the bodies of cacti, sucking the sap and exuding a sticky substance, which encourages sooty mould.

Thrips – thrips, particularly western flower thrips, are an increasing problem in collections. These tiny insects can be seen running about on the petals of flowers and are very hard to kill. In addition to damaged and deformed flowers, they are also blamed for causing damage to plant bodies, similar to that caused by red spider mite.

Vine weevils – the larvae of vine weevils are large cream-coloured grubs with brown heads. They enter the body of plants at or below soil level and then proceed to eat them hollow. After the infestation has been eradicated, especially if the damage is extensive, it may be necessary to cut away the entire damaged area and treat the remainder of the plant as a cutting. Periodic treatment with a specifically targeted insecticide should prevent an infestation.

Other pests – there are many other pests that can cause problems. Some succulents attract aphids, or whitefly. Slugs and snails can eat the

all about cacti and succulents

growing points out of the softer-bodied cacti (e.g. rebutias). Rodents can also be a nuisance. Vigilance, followed by prompt and thorough treatment, is the only sure way of avoiding major problems.

WARNING: Insecticides are designed to kill insects, but they can also kill humans. Always follow the manufacturer's instructions regarding the use and storage of chemicals and take precautions to provide good ventilation and skin protection.

BELOW: Rebutia and Sulcorebutia plants are rewarding and easy to grow, but watch out for red spider mites.

the cacti handbook

Diseases

Diseases tend to be less of a concern than pests, particularly if a good clean 'housekeeping' regime is adopted. Remove and dispose of dead plants or parts of plants, do not allow fallen leaves, or other detritus, to accumulate and clean up spillages of compost. In addition, the provision of adequate ventilation and air movement should ensure disease does not present a major problem.

The diseases most likely to be encountered are:

Rot (wet) – if a plant suddenly goes soft, or collapses, it is probably suffering from rot. This often occurs when a plant has lost its roots due to over-watering, or if an open wound (a cut or otherwise damaged surface) has got wet or infected. Provided it is caught early enough, it may be possible to salvage at least part of the plant. Cut the plant back until only healthy tissue is left – all the soft, brownish, mushy rot must be completely removed, otherwise it will

LEFT: Huernia confusa – Stapeliads are particularly prone to damage and rot in cold and/or damp conditions.

all about cacti and succulents

ABOVE: Thelocactus bicolor – sooty mould, if not controlled, will spoil the appearance of thelocactus plants.

quickly spread through the rest of the plant. Treat the healthy portion as a cutting. Always sterilise the knife between cuts to prevent the transfer of rot to the healthy tissue.

Rot (dry) – unlike with wet rot, the plant does not turn to mush; instead it slowly dries out and goes rubbery, with bright orange-brown discoloration of the tissues. A similar problem occurs with Stapeliads, but the discoloration is black. Treat the plant as for wet rot.

Botrytis – this grey fungal growth can sometimes be seen on plants, but unless they are being grown in particularly cool, dank and humid conditions, it is more likely to form on dead material, such as rotten plants or old flower remains. Always remove dead flowers, leaves and seedpods before the winter to prevent botrytis getting established on them and progressing into the plant itself.

Sooty mould – this black mould is a common problem on some cacti, particularly ferocactus, hamatocactus and thelocactus species, which secrete a sugary nectar from glands on their areoles. It is unsightly and difficult to remove. Wash the secretions off the plant during the growing season to try to prevent the mould forming.

Other Damage

Finally, it is worth mentioning a few common forms of damage that can disfigure otherwise healthy plants:

Scorch – although subject to high temperatures, many desert plants in their natural environment grow in the shade of rocks, trees, etc. and are cooled by the wind. Plants in cultivation that are grown under glass can easily become scorched. This can be prevented by the provision of adequate ventilation and air movement.

Splitting – when cacti are watered, their bodies swell and become firmer to the touch. Some, such as notocactus, turbinicarpus and lophophora, are prone to splitting if given too much water. To minimise the risk, give reduced quantities of water for the first couple of waterings after the plant's winter rest. Do not suddenly try to increase the growth rate of a plant that has previously been grown slowly.

Root loss – a plant that is not growing when it should, or is slowly shrivelling, is probably not getting water and nourishment into its stem. It may simply need more water, but before doing so it is worth checking the plant closely. Unfortunately, the symptoms for lack of water are the same as those indicating a problem with the root system, which is preventing water being taken up into the plant itself. In the case of cacti and succulents, this problem is most often caused by over-watering and

all about cacti and succulents

results in root loss. In which case, the addition of more water could be catastrophic. If a plant is found to have lost most or all of its roots, remove any unhealthy remnants using a sharp, sterile knife, and treat the cut surfaces with fungicide powder. The plant should then be treated as a cutting until a new root system becomes established.

Physical damage – all plants will be damaged if they are mistreated or handled incorrectly. Care should be taken to avoid cutting, bruising or tearing plants when handling them. Some succulents (e.g. some echeverias) have a powdery farinose coating on the leaves, which is easily rubbed off when touched. Cacti are prone to losing spine clusters if they are not handled gently during repotting, particularly if gloves are worn. This is especially a problem for hook-spined plants (e.g. Mammillaria bocasana), where the central spine is shaped like a fishhook and readily catches onto flesh, clothes, etc. Such damage is not usually fatal but will spoil the appearance of the plant.

RIGHT: Rebutia tarvitaensis – a seedling dwarfed by its flower; the plant is only about 2 cm (0.75 in) in diameter.

Increasing the Size of Your Collection

Be warned – collecting cacti and succulents can be addictive! Once you start, your biggest problem will be finding room to house your ever-growing collection.

In the past many plants were collected from their natural habitat. Although this still happens – often illegally – the importance of conservation is now more generally accepted. Apart from the moral considerations, plants that have been uprooted and exported have a much worse survival rate than those propagated in cultivation.

Many plants are bought from shops, garden centres or nurseries. Shops and garden centres frequently only sell a small range of cacti and succulents. In addition, their plants are often unlabelled – or worse, incorrectly labelled. Also they may not have been looked after properly and so, if they have been on the shelf for a long time, their health may have deteriorated. Beware of the practice of attaching artificial flowers to the plants; this invariably causes damage, in extreme cases leading to infection and the death of the plant. Plants from specialist nurseries will usually be of good quality and be well cared for, but they may be more expensive. These nurseries will also often sell the harder-to-find plants. Mail order specialists can be a convenient way of acquiring plants not otherwise available locally. The ability of cacti and succulents to survive bare-rooted, without water, makes them better suited to postal travel than many plants, but there are disadvantages. Particularly the cost of postage and the fact that you cannot see the size and health of the plant until it arrives.

If buying plants from abroad you must check the applicable, restrictions and paperwork. Remember that plants imported from hot climates may struggle to get established.

The cheapest and most rewarding method of acquiring plants is by growing them from seed. Costs are minimal and can be offset by the trading of surplus seedlings. Patience is required though – seed raising will not quickly provide a mature collection of specimen cacti. Probably the best source of plants – and the quickest way to gain

RIGHT: Hoya cinnamomifolia – many hoya species are rarely found in garden centres and often have to be obtained via mail order.

knowledge is via a Cactus and Succulent Society. Most countries have such a society and, if there is a group local to you, they may sell plants at very reasonable prices. As enthusiasts will have cultivated them, these plants tend to be well cared for and will be accompanied by free advice on how to look after them. Don't be afraid to join a specialist society; it is not necessary to be an experienced grower, most societies are very welcoming and the benefits can be enormous.

BELOW: Some growers specialise almost exclusively in just one genus, such as mammillaria.

part two: cactus directory

the cacti handbook

How to use the directory

There are so many species of cacti that it is impossible to include pictures of them all in this book. A few large books do attempt to give a fairly comprehensive coverage, but even they cannot claim to illustrate all of them.

The pictures included here have been selected to help a beginner gain a basic appreciation of the different genera, and to help in choosing the plants he or she may wish to grow. To that end, the picture choice is based largely on two criteria:

- those genera and species that are most likely to be readily obtainable and that beginners are most likely to be successful growing

- an attempt to show a range of the forms within the larger genera

Clearly these two criteria are not always compatible and so a few of the harder-to-find plants have also been included. A small number of more 'specialist' plants have been included to provide a slightly more

cactus directory

comprehensive coverage, yet many others that are easy to grow, but not really suitable for small collections (e.g. selenicereus, hylocereus, pereskia, etc.) have been omitted. Many of the pictures show relatively small, fairly young, flowering plants. This is intended to provide encouragement to the grower and to dispel the myths about the age and size that cacti need to be before they will flower. The descriptions and the four cultivation symbols will help provide an awareness of any special features of the plants, particularly with respect to cultivation requirements.

Cultivation Symbols

Light

 Full sun Plenty of sunshine, while ensuring good air movement to avoid scorching.

 Partial shade Indirect sunlight or partial shade.

 Shade A shady location is preferred.

Winter Temperature

 Give winter heat Tender; provide added heat in winter to maintain a minimum temperature of about 10°C (50°F).

 Keep frost free For safety it is wise to keep this plant frost free. Maintain a minimum temperature of about 5°C (40°F).

 Frost tolerant Provided it is kept dry, this plant should safely withstand frost.

cactus directory

Compost

 Normal - Use standard, free-draining compost (see p. 20).

 Free draining - Extra drainage needed; add extra grit to the standard mixture.

 Calcareous - Use a calcareous compost. It can be made by adding about 1 part limestone chippings to 6 parts of the standard mixture. Additional grit should be also added for extra drainage.

 Added humus - Add additional humus material (e.g. peat leafmould, or similar).

Amount of water to be given during the growing period

 Above average Give plenty of water, but avoid waterlogging.

 Average Water thoroughly, but allow the plant to dry out completely between waterings.

 Below average Water sparingly.

Acanthocalycium violaceum

Commonly used synonyms: Current thinking suggests that Acanthocalycium violaceum should at most be a form of the less impressive *A. spiniflorum*. It is also very occasionally seen as *Echinopsis violacea*.

Country of origin: Argentina

Almost any of the acanthocalycium species are worth growing, but this is the one most frequently seen, and deservedly so. Its freely produced lilac flowers make a lovely show once the plants reach approximately 5 cm (2 in) in diameter. Cultivation presents no particular difficulty, although freezing temperatures should be avoided.

Aporocactus flagelliformis

Commonly used synonyms: Sometimes known as the Rat's Tail Cactus because of its growth habit, efforts are now being made to rename it *Disocactus flagelliformis*.

Country of origin: Mexico

Probably because of its epiphytic origins, *A. flagelliformis* seems to prefer growing in porches, or even indoor locations, to greenhouses. Too much sunlight in the summer certainly seems to be detrimental.

Many growers seem to believe that because it is an epiphyte it requires high winter temperatures, yet experience has shown that it can survive freezing without harm, if it is completely dry.

Crested forms are occasionally available, as is a rather interesting monstrose form that does not have the trailing habit; instead it forms upright pyramids of profusely produced offsets.

the cacti handbook

Aporophyllum hybrids

Country of origin: Nursery cultivated

A large number of these hybrid cacti has been produced by artificially crossing aporocacti with other epiphytes, particularly epiphyllums. Generally, they share the characteristics of the two parents, having larger, showier blooms than an aporocactus, but still retaining the pendant trailing habit – albeit usually with somewhat stiffer branches.

They are not commonly seen for sale, except from specialist sources, but they are worth seeking out. The plant shown is *Aporophyllum* 'Wendy', but most of the named hybrids are worth growing. The choice is simply a matter of personal preference with regard to flower colour.

cactus directory

Ariocarpus species

Country of origin: Mexico & southern USA

The various ariocarpus species (which include plants formerly given the old generic names of neogomesia and roseocactus) are often considered to be plants for the experienced grower and are seldom sold in non-specialist outlets. They are included here to provide awareness of this fascinating group of plants.

That said, provided a very careful control is maintained with regard to watering, they are not really as difficult to grow as their reputation might suggest. They are, however, extremely slow growing, so great patience is required – particularly if they are grown from seed.

Astrophytum capricorne

Country of origin: Mexico

Astrophytum capricorne and the related – some say synonymous – A. senile are quite variable in respect of the number and length of the spines and the extent of the flock markings on the body. Some plants have little or no marking at all.

The various species of astrophytum are quite readily available on the market. Only *A. asterias* is consistently difficult to grow well. The others present no real problems, as long they are not given too much water and they get plenty of sunshine – with air movement to prevent scorching. Alkaline compost is preferable.

cactus directory

Astrophytum myriostigma

Country of origin: Mexico

Astrophytum myriostigma is the most common astrophytum species in cultivation. There are a number of forms, some of which – *A. columnare* and *A. coahuilense* – have been treated as separate species. Others, such as *A. nudum* and *A. quadricostatum*, are often considered to be varieties. The latter has four ribs instead of the more usual five, although many a cherished plant sprouts a fifth rib when it gets older. In fact, this plant can develop as many as eight ribs. As with *A. capricorne*, the amount of patterning on the body can range from almost none to heavy covering.

The plant shown is unusual in that it has formed a large clump of smallish heads. Like all astrophytum species, *A. myriostigma* normally remains solitary unless damaged or grafted. Lovely yellow flowers are produced in the summer.

Astrophytum – Japanese cultivar

Country of origin: Nursery cultivated

Japanese nurserymen have bred a number of extremely heavily patterned forms of the various astrophytum species. The best known is a form of *A. asterias* called 'Super Kabuto'. Like the plant shown, these cultivars are almost always grafted.

Although not representative of the true species in habitat, these spectacular forms are highly sought after by collectors.

The plant pictured is a cultivar of *A. myriostigma*.

cactus directory

Astrophytum ornatum

Country of origin: Mexico

A. ornatum is the largest growing of the astrophytum species. In habitat it can reach more than 1 m (3 ft) tall and is reputed, in rare cases, to reach nearly three times that height. In cultivation it will usually remain rather smaller.

Astrophytum species are not easy to re-root if they lose their roots. This, and their tendency to remain solitary, means that they cannot readily be propagated from cuttings; so most plants are seed raised. Astrophytum seed should be handled carefully as it crushes easily and must be sown soon after harvesting, when it is as fresh as possible.

Borzicactus aureispinus

Commonly used synonyms: *Hildewintera aureispina, Cleistocactus aureispinus, Cleistocactus winteri.*

Country of origin: Bolivia

Best grown in a hanging pot, its trailing stems will eventually require it to be moved to a large hanging basket. As it gets larger, its arching golden-spined stems make *Borzicactus aureispinus* a most attractive plant. The orange flowers become increasingly freely produced and can occur in succession throughout the year.

It should be grown in a sunny position. When combined with a high location in a greenhouse, this should maintain it in good condition, without having to provide excessive heat. Some growers advocate giving occasional small amounts of water on warm days throughout the winter to help prevent die back of older stems.

cactus directory

Cephalocereus senilis

Country of origin: Mexico

This wonderful, white, hairy cactus slowly grows into an impressive columnar plant. Although in habitat it can reach up to 15 m (50 ft) in height, it will be a long time before it outgrows its welcome in cultivation.

The plant is usually grown for its appearance, as most growers will not get to see its yellowish, nocturnal flowers in cultivation.

It should be grown in a sunny position and, as the plant gets older, increased care should be taken not to over-water it.

Cereus group – Carnegia gigantea

Country of origin: Southern USA

The immense, tall-growing nature of most species of cereus and similar genera (e.g. pachycereus and some trichocereus and stenocereus) means they are unsuitable for most growers. They are ideal for outdoor plantings in warm countries or as a backdrop in larger greenhouses until they outgrow their welcome. Most, however, are not suitable for consideration in this book. However, they are an important group of cacti, so three examples are included.

The picture of *Carnegia gigantea*, commonly called Saguaro, clearly shows why many of these plants cannot be grown in confined spaces. They grow very slowly, but can reach over 15 m (50 ft) in height and weigh as much as 10 tonnes. The photograph was taken in central Arizona.

cactus directory

Cereus group – blue-stemmed species

Country of origin: South America

Although in time they will become too tall for most collections, some species are sufficiently eye-catching and beautiful to warrant growing. These are the blue-stemmed species, such as some species of browningia, cephalocereus, pilocereus and pilosocereus. The most impressive are those with contrasting gold spines, or those whose spines are accompanied by white hairs.

Care is needed to grow these plants well in cultivation. Most blue-bodied species are sensitive to low temperatures and require extra heat in winter. The blue appearance comes from a farinose covering, which requires bright sunlight to form to its full effect. It is easily marked by touch or by being sprayed with water or insecticide.

Cereus group – Cereus peruvianus

Country of origin: Argentina and Brazil

The origins of this cactus are uncertain, due in part to its widespread cultivation for fencing and as a source of wood. Its normal form is not particularly interesting to collectors, but there is a monstrose form that is readily available. This grows slowly and stays quite small, with a multitude of growing points, forming a fascinating oddity. Given enough time and root room it may eventually reach 85 cm (33 in) in height, but that would be exceptional in indoor collections.

cactus directory

Chamaecereus silvestrii

Commonly used synonyms: Although *Lobivia silvestrii* is generally accepted as being the correct name for this plant, it is still often labelled under its established name of *Chamaecereus silvestrii*.

Country of origin: Argentina

Often disregarded by experienced growers, who seek rarity and challenge, this plant must be one of the easiest and most rewarding a beginner can grow. It produces soft, loosely attached stems, keeping low and spreading sideways to fill the pot. If given the correct conditions it will produce masses of orange-red blooms each spring.

Although it will tolerate most growing conditions, to maximise flowering it should be grown in the sunniest position possible and – provided it is kept completely dry – given as cold a winter rest as possible.

Chamaelobivia hybrids

Country of origin: Nursery cultivated

Usually labelled *Chamaelobivia*, and sometimes followed by a cultivar name, these hybrid cacti have been produced by artificially crossing *Chamaecereus silvestrii* with other lobivia species. They usually take the form of a stronger version of the branching stems of *C. silvestri*, and although the plant shown has similar coloured flowers to this parent, the introduction of other lobivias has led to a wide variety of flower colours and sizes.

'Purist' growers often scorn hybrids and cultivars, but if you are looking for ease of growth and spectacular flowers, they are certainly worthy of consideration.

cactus directory

Cleistocactus strausii

Country of origin: Argentina & Bolivia

As long as space allows, variety and height will make a cactus collection more interesting. The acquisition of C. strausii is certainly recommended for that purpose.

Given good light, this readily obtainable plant grows quite quickly, producing a tall, white-spined column up to 8 cm (3 in) diameter and 1.5 m (5 ft) or more in height – up to 3 m (10 ft) if planted in a outdoor bed. Eventually it will produce offsets from near the base. These side shoots will grow upwards, parallel with the original stem.

Plants in excess of 60 cm (2 ft) in height can be expected to produce tubular, maroon flowers.

Cleistocactus candelilla

Country of origin: Bolivia

Not all the species of *Cleistocactus* grow as tall, or as straight, as *C. strausii*. Many have much smaller-diameter stems and some sprawl and need support. Several of these less impressive species compensate by flowering at a younger age. *C. santacruzensis*, in particular, is reputed to flower when still quite small.

Cleistocactus are not difficult to grow from seed. This is probably just as well because, although *C. strausii* is readily available, sadly – despite their attractions – all too few of the other species are offered for sale, except by a few specialist nurseries.

cactus directory

Copiapoa hypogaea

Commonly used synonyms: *Copiapoa barquitensis.*

Country of origin: Chile

In common with several of the other small-growing copiapoa species, *C. hypogaea* flowers readily in cultivation. It will produce a succession of yellow flowers from a fairly early age. Its brown clumping body shows off the white, woolly tuft on its areoles. *C. humilis* is another small-growing, free-flowering species. It tends to produce more smaller offsets and less white wool – although it is very variable.

Although copiapoa species appreciate sunlight, they are prone to scorch and so good ventilation, as well as a partially shaded position, is recommended. However, too dark a location must be avoided.

Copiapoa krainziana

Commonly used synonyms: *Copiapoa scopulina*.

Country of origin: Chile

Copiapoa krainziana can be reluctant to flower in collections, but it is worth growing because it looks good all year round. Its white, hair-like spination makes it a most attractive addition to a collection.

Large clumps of *C. krainziana* and the other larger-growing species, such as the grey-bodied *C. cinerea*, need care in cultivation, but can eventually make fine specimens. Care with watering and plenty of air movement all year round is recommended.

cactus directory

Coryphantha species

Country of origin: Mexico & southern USA

Coryphantha species are closely related to mammillaria and escobaria, the latter having been combined with them by some taxonomists. The three plants shown were acquired with three different names, but in all probability they are all forms of *C. elephantidens*. The spination of some of the other species varies quite considerably from the plants in the photograph.

Although a few coryphantha species have pink flowers, most have yellow. They are usually globular plants, offsetting and clustering with age. They produce loose, white wool that accumulates at their crown, giving them a very attractive appearance.

Some species are tuberous rooted and they must be given a suitably deep pot. All species prefer alkaline compost.

Echinocactus grusonii

Country of origin: Mexico

Virtually extinct in habitat due to dam construction, the 'Golden Barrel' is hugely popular in cultivation, particularly in botanical gardens where plants that have been bedded out thrive and look very spectacular.

Although they are slow growing, with patience you can produce large, globular plants covered in spectacular, fierce, golden spines and a loose, woolly deposit in the crown. The relatively small, yellow flowers are unlikely to be seen on plants grown in pots. However, the flowers are readily produced on mature plants grown outside in beds in warm countries.

E. grusonii have surprisingly small, shallow root systems for their size and so should be planted in shallow pans, rather than in normal-depth pots. They can be prone to marking if subjected to low temperatures

cactus directory

Echinocereus engelmannii

Country of origin: Mexico & southern USA

A huge number of different echinocereus species are offered for sale. The echinocereus species shown have been selected to show the significant variation in appearance between different species. *E. engelmannii*, with its large pink-purple flowers and green stigmas, is representative of several of the more commonly seen species.

In cultivation *E. engelmannii* will eventually form a good-sized clump, but nothing like plants in habitat, which can reach almost 1 m (40 in) across. As with many of the more open-bodied species of Echinocereus, a sunny position is best. However, these plants are prone to scorching if insufficient air movement is provided.

the cacti handbook

Echinocereus huitcholensis

Commonly used synonyms: *Echinocereus plomosus, Echinocereus polyacanthus v. huitcholensis.*

Country of origin: Mexico

Echinocereus huitcholensis is often circulated with the field collection number LAU 768. Its inclusion here represents similar plants, such as *E. salm-dyckianus* and *E. acifer*, with their stunning, long-tubed, orange-red flowers.

Perhaps less easy to obtain than the more typical pink-flowered echinocereus species, these plants are worth the effort needed to acquire them. They should start to flower while still quite small.

cactus directory

Echinocereus pentalophus

Commonly used synonyms: Historical confusion has left many misnamed plants of *E. pentalophus*, along with its Mexican and Texan subspecies, and the similar *E. berlandieri*. The erroneous name *E. blankii* has added to the confusion.

Country of origin: Mexico

The large, funnel-shaped flowers with their pale throats more than compensate for the space needed to accommodate the plant's sprawling stems. These have the annoying habit of overhanging the pot and getting in the way of – or even damaging – adjacent plants.

Echinocereus poselgeri

Commonly used synonyms: *Wilcoxia poselgeri, Wilcoxia tuberosa.*

Country of origin: Mexico & southern USA

Although it is now accepted that the plants contained in the old genus of wilcoxia are, in fact, species of echinocereus, the old name tends to persist. This is probably because of their distinctive pencil-thin stems and tuberous root systems.

As with any tuberous rooted cactus, care should be taken to avoid damage to the tuber, and the risk of rot should be taken seriously. That said, they are not particularly difficult to grow and their long, thin stems make a change from the more common clumping, or globular, cacti.

cactus directory

Echinocereus rigidissimus

Country of origin: Mexico & southern USA

This cristate form of *E. rigidissimus* is occasionally offered for sale. Although unlikely to flower in cultivation, it makes a beautiful specimen with its very fine spination and convoluted body.

As with any cristate cactus, care must be taken to avoid watering from the top, as moisture can remain in the folds of the plant body, with the resultant risk of rot.

Echinocereus rigidissimus ssp. rubispinus

Commonly used synonyms: *Echinocereus pectinatus v. rubispinus*

Country of origin: Mexico

E. rigidissimus is quite common in the southern states of the USA, but this subspecies comes only from Mexico. The tighter, more strongly coloured spination makes it more attractive than its relative. As a further bonus, it is reputed to be more free-flowering in cultivation, readily producing its large, pale-throated, pink flowers.

A large number of cacti warrant a closer examination than many people give them. The colours and patterns of this plant's growing tip and/or a small area of the spination can be quite wonderful.

cactus directory

Echinocereus subinermis

Country of origin: Mexico

Most echinocereus species have either pink or scarlet flowers, but it is worth searching out one of the relatively few yellow-flowered species. *E. subinermis* is a good example and *E. stoloniferous* is another.

As can be seen, the flowers are large and showy. They are freely produced, with the flowers dwarfing the body of younger plants. These plants are usually solitary but can eventually offset. However, they tend to remain fairly compact, adding to their attraction in cultivation.

Echinopsis species

Country of origin: Argentina, Bolivia, Brazil & Paraguay

Many growers start their collection with an echinopsis cutting, usually *E. multiplex, E. eyriesii, E. oxygona* or one of the other white or pale pink flowered species.

These extremely undemanding, clumping plants are not the most interesting of species when not in flower, but their long, scented, tubular flowers are spectacular. Once the furry buds start to develop and flowering approaches, they grow at a seemingly impossible rate. The flowers can be up to 18 cm (7 in) long and 10 cm (4 in) in diameter. Unfortunately, they open in late evening and will, at best, only last through the following day and a second night before wilting.

Bringing the plants into flower should not be difficult, providing they are given good light and a very cold, dry winter rest.

cactus directory

Echinopsis ancistrophora

Country of origin: Argentina & Bolivia

E. ancistrophora has several varieties and includes a number of plants that previously had their own names. The plant shown can be found labelled *E. leucorhodantha* or *Pseudolobivia leucorhodantha*. The now obsolete genus, pseudolobivia, contains day-flowering plants, often with richly coloured flowers. Cultivation of pseudolobivia is no different from that of echinopsis.

Echinopsis mamillosa v. kermesina

Commonly used synonyms: *Pseudolobivia kermesina, Echinopsis kermesina.*

Country of origin: Bolivia

The dramatic, deeply coloured flowers of *E. mamillosa v. kermesina* tend to take the form of a slightly downward-curved funnel. Older plants have a tendency to 'slump' down on themselves and to mark towards the base. This plant tends to grow a larger diameter body and is less prone to clumping than the typical echinopsis.

cactus directory

Echinopsis obrepanda v. callichroma

Commonly used synonyms: The name of this plant has been the subject of debate over the years. It has appeared as *Pseudolobivia obrepanda v. callichroma*, *Echinopsis callichroma* and *E. obrepanda v. purpurea*, among others.

Country of origin: Bolivia

The plant shown is little more than a seedling in a 5cm (2in) square pot, yet even at that small size it has produced a spectacular bloom at least 18 cm (7 in) in length.

Echinopsis hybrids

Country of origin: Nursery cultivated

In addition to the many beautiful echinopsis species there are a large number of echinopsis hybrids in cultivation. They have been carefully bred over many years by selecting the largest, best coloured and/or scented flowers. Although some people think that only true species should be grown, these hybrids are highly sought after by growers who are more interested in the beautiful and the spectacular than the 'pure'. Perhaps the most famous of these are the Paramount hybrids and the Schick hybrids from California.

The plant shown was acquired with the label *Echinopsis 'Rosaflora'*, but its origins are uncertain.

cactus directory

Epiphyllum cooperi

Commonly used synonym: *Epiphyllum crenatum*

Country of origin: Guatemala, Honduras & Mexico

Most growers' collections include a few epiphyllum plants. At least they do until the plants become too large and their ever-increasing demand upon the available growing space relegates them to dark corners of the greenhouse before they are ousted altogether. This is unfortunate because – although they do become large and their sprawling leaves are not very attractive – when they flower they are stunning.

Only a few 'true' species are in widespread cultivation. Perhaps the best is *E. cooperi*, which produces large – 15 cm (6 in) diameter – whitish flowers. These open on summer evenings and fill the greenhouse with scent. Unlike many night-opening flowers they usually remain open the following day.

Epiphyllum hybrids

Commonly used synonyms: *Epicactus hybrids, orchid cactus.*

Country of origin: Nursery cultivated

Although there are few epiphyllum species in cultivation, there are hundreds of hybrids available. These have been bred to enhance the flowers, usually in terms of size – up to 30 cm (12 in) in diameter – or colour (white, yellow, orange, red, pink and purple). The petals of some flowers have an almost metallic sheen. Different growers have different tastes so just acquire what catches your eye. The plant shown is labelled 'Space Rocket', although its blooms are slightly smaller than would normally be expected for this particular cultivar. Epiphyllums require partial shade, but will tolerate quite heavy shading. They should be kept warm in winter.

cactus directory

Epithelantha micromeris

Country of origin: Mexico & southern USA

Although they will occasionally offset, these miniature plants usually remain solitary. They will never outgrow their welcome as they grow slowly and often will not exceed 5 cm (2 in) in diameter. The large plant shown is exceptional.

Given favourable conditions they will flower readily, though the pale-pink flowers are small and – unlike their larger and more impressive seedpods – do not show up well against the dense white spination of the plant.

The growing point tends to be sunken, with a tuft of new growth in the centre, giving the plant an interesting and distinctive appearance.

Espostoa melanostele

Country of origin: Peru

One of the attractions of a mixed cactus collection is variety of appearance. Many cacti are globular, or form low-growing mounds, so the addition of some columnar plants adds greatly to the overall effect. Espostoa species are especially valuable in this respect because of their covering of white woolly hairs.

Flowers are rare in cultivation. Some species can be as tall as 5 m (16 ft) in habitat and so take a long time to reach maturity. The spines on *E. melanostele* protrude through the wool, but this is not the case with all species. However, the spines are there, waiting to impale the unwary grower who gets too close to the plant's soft wool.

cactus directory

Escobaria minima

Commonly used synonyms: *Escobaria nellieae, Coryphantha minima, Coryphantha nellieae.*

Country of origin: Southern USA

Escobaria minima is a gem of a plant from Texas. Sadly, like so many of the choicest plants, it is very slow growing and not the easiest to keep alive. A clump, grown on its own roots, of more than 10 cm (4 in) in diameter will probably be quite old. Its tight spination covers the small stems, but to see it at its best, it should be covered with its pinkish-purple flowers.

the cacti handbook

Escobaria strobiliformis

Country of origin: Mexico & southern USA

Other than *E. minima*, most of the escobaria species offered for sale – and that is not many, in Britain at least – are very similar. Although the stem size varies and some cluster, while others remain solitary, most stay small, are covered with straight, pure white spines, and produce a steady succession of smallish, pale-pink flowers. They are not particularly eye-catching as part of a large collection, but they are pleasant when looked at individually.

Although not universally accepted, many growers advocate the use of calcareous compost for these plants.

cactus directory

Ferocactus acanthodes

Commonly used synonyms: The plant pictured was acquired as *Ferocactus acanthodes*, but is more likely to be the variety *eastwoodiae*, also known as *F. eastwoodiae* or *F. cylindraceus v. eastwoodiae*.

Country of origin: Mexico & southern USA

Although there are one or two exceptions, most ferocactus species are slightly reluctant to flower in cultivation. They certainly will not do so until they have reached a significant size – after several years at least. Notwithstanding, they remain popular, probably because of their fierce spination, which makes them stereotypical of the image of a globular cactus.

Ferocactus acanthodes is usually solitary. Offsetting at a small size, as seen here, is most unusual and is possibly the result of earlier damage to the growing point.

the cacti handbook

Ferocactus gracilis v. coloratus

Commonly used synonyms: *Ferocactus coloratus.*

Country of origin: Mexico

When grown in good light *Ferocactus gracilis v. coloratus* produces wonderful, stout, red spines. To see them at their best the plant should be lightly misted with water and viewed in sunlight, when the spines glow with colour.

On warm days during the growing season, it is a good idea to spray ferocactus species regularly with clean water. This helps disperse the sugary secretion produced by glands above the areoles. If left, it will attract black sooty mould and spoil the appearance of the plant.

cactus directory

Ferocactus wislizenii

Country of origin: Mexico & southern USA

Ferocactus wislizenii is one of the larger-growing ferocactus species. In habitat – such as this one photographed in Arizona – it regularly grows as tall as 1 m (40 in), and sometimes taller. In cultivation, it is not likely to grow that large, but will steadily mature into a fierce, but handsome, specimen.

Ferocactus species are worthy additions to any collection, particularly the smaller-growing and earlier-flowering ones, such as *F. fordii*, although they are less often seen for sale than their larger relatives.

Frailea grahliana

Country of origin: Argentina & Paraguay

It is commonly believed that the flowers of frailea species do not open. In some cases that is true, and certainly they do not need to open to be pollinated, but in others – such as the plant shown, which is most probably *F. grahliana* – they will open if the conditions are correct. High temperatures seem to be the trigger, more so even than direct sunlight.

Contrary to their rather unpopular reputation, most frailea species are easy to grow, remain small, and are attractive when their flowers do open fully.

cactus directory

Gymnocalycium baldianum

Commonly used synonyms: *Gymnocalycium venturianum*

Country of origin: Argentina

Gymnocalycium species are deservedly popular in cultivation. In general, they are undemanding, present few cultivation difficulties and flower very reliably. Many are relatively easily to obtain, although a few are seen less often.

When selecting species to grow, it is worth looking for those with different coloured flowers. Most gymnocalycium have cream or pink flowers, so species, such as *G. baldianum*, *G. tillianum* and *G. carminanthum*, with red flowers make a pleasing change.

G. baldianum is usually seen as a solitary plant, but it may eventually clump with age.

Gymnocalycium damsii v. tucavocense

Country of origin: Bolivia

With its pink flowers, *Gymnocalycium damsii v. tucavocense* is rather prettier than *G. damsii*. Even when not in flower, its clustering purple and green bodies make it very attractive.

As with most gymnocalycium species, a little shade from the hottest sun is advisable, and the provision of an acid substrate is welcomed. Some growers recommend giving winter warmth and a touch of moisture throughout the year, but they seem to survive without problem when kept dry but frost free in the colder months.

cactus directory

Gymnocalycium gibbosum v. nobile

Country of origin: Argentina

There seems to be some doubt as to whether this variety should exist separately from *Gymnocalycium gibbosum*. The name refers to larger forms that have stronger spines than is usual for *G. gibbosum*.

These plants tend to be solitary. Although some have reddish flowers, others – such as the plant shown – have white flowers of a rather cleaner colour than many of the off-white or cream flowers frequently seen on gymnocalycium species. Gymnocalycium species are all recognisable by their distinctive smoth, scaly buds.

Gymnocalycium horridispinum

Commonly used synonyms: *Gymnocalycium monvillei ssp. horridispinum.*

Country of origin: Argentina

Gymnocalycium horridispinum has very strong spination, particularly as the plant gets older. Its flowers range from white with pink-edged petals to a deep pink or mauve.

Although somewhat variable, *G. horridispinum* often has a brownish body. This is typical of a number of gymnocalycium species; others have body colours ranging from light to dark green – some matt, some glossy – through to pink or even purplish.

cactus directory

Gymnocalycium mihanovichii

Commonly used synonyms: Historically, there has been confusion between *Gymnocalycium mihanovichii* and the similar *G. friedrichii*.

Country of origin: Paraguay

This small-growing plant is often one of the first cacti bought by growers. It is often seen for sale, complete with its distinctively shaped buds which can be yellowish, white or even brownish, although very often they are pink.

G. mihanovichii is the parent of a number of gaudily coloured forms called 'Hibotan', which originated in Japan. Their bodies can be a single bright colour, or a variegated combination of pinks, yellows and browns. Their lack of chlorophyll means they cannot survive without being grafted. Care should be taken with them as they are often grafted onto a very cold-sensitive Hylocereus stock.

the cacti handbook

Gymnocalycium uruguayense

Country of origin: Uruguay

As mentioned previously, gymnocalycium species with unusually coloured flowers tend to be highly sought after. *G. uruguayense*, like *G. andreae* and *G. leeanum*, has yellow flowers. To be more accurate, it may have yellow flowers, as this clumping species is quite variable and can also have white or pink flowers. The yellow ones are, of course, the most popular.

cactus directory

Haageocereus species

Country of origin: Chile & Peru

Although not a particularly popular genus, haageocereus plants are worth a second look if seen offered for sale. Although they are reluctant to flower in cultivation in more temperate countries, the dense spination, often in attractive shades of yellow or reddish brown, make them useful plants to give variety to a collection of cacti.

The choice of species to grow is based largely on availability and personal preference of spine colour. The plant shown was acquired with the name *H. divaricatispinus*. However, as with many haageocereus seen for sale, there is some doubt over the accuracy of the labelling.

Although most seem able to tolerate frost-free conditions, a little extra heat in winter would be welcomed, as would mineral-based compost.

Hamatocactus setispinus

Commonly used synonyms: *Thelocactus setispinus, Ferocactus setispinus, Echinocactus setispinus.*

Country of origin: Mexico & southern USA

H. setispinus, whose habitat straddles the border between Texas and Mexico, is well worth seeking out and growing. It flowers freely, even when quite young, and produces a succession of silky, yellow flowers with red throats throughout the summer months. The flowers are followed by the production of bright red seedpods.

Like its ferocactus relatives it is prone to sooty mould. This forms on the sugary secretions, which ooze from near the areoles and will disfigure the plant if not removed regularly with clean water.

Leuchtenbergia principis

Country of origin: Mexico

L. principis is easily recognisable by its very long, thin, angled tubercles – so pronounced that some specimens appear to be all tubercle and no body – and its twisted, papery spines.

It is easy to propagate from fresh seed and is not especially difficult to grow. It develops a significant taproot and so must be grown in a deep pot. The only real problem with cultivation is the tendency for its tubercles to die back if it is given insufficient water during the growing season. However, too much water can lead to the roots rotting. To minimise the risk, the compost, as well as being calcareous, must be very free draining. Flowering tends to be later in the summer than for most cacti.

Lobivia arachnacantha

Commonly used synonyms: *Echinopsis arachnacantha, Lobivia ancistrophora v. arachnacantha.*

Country of origin: Bolivia

There is currently a move to absorb the entire lobivia genus into echinopsis. Although this seems to be generally accepted by botanists, it is less popular with growers and so the lobivia name still regularly appears on plant labels. For that reason it has been retained here.

Almost any lobivia seen offered for sale deserves consideration, if it is flowers that you want. *L. arachnacantha* does not have the most stunning flowers of the genus, but they are attractive, and the plant's small growth habit and tidy spination add to its appeal.

cactus directory

Lobivia chrysochete

Commonly used synonyms: *Echinopsis chrysochete.*

Country of origin: Argentina & Bolivia

Lobivia chrysochete and its named varieties freely produce red or orange flowers, some shades of which seem to glow. As with the other lobivia species included here – but unlike the plants in the older, narrower genus of echinopsis – this is a day-flowering species.

Lobivias are generally undemanding, but appreciate an acid substrate and air movement to prevent scorch.

Lobivia haematantha v. densispina

Commonly used synonyms: *Lobivia densispina, Lobivia famatimensis, Echinopsis densispina.*

Country of origin: Argentina

Lobivia haematantha v. densispina is another free-flowering plant with neat spination. Sadly, like so many others, it suffers from a great deal of confusion and disagreement regarding its correct taxonomy.

For best flower production lobivia species should be given a good sunny position and a cold, completely dry winter rest. Watering should not commence in the spring until flower buds are well developed. Water too soon and you risk the buds aborting.

cactus directory

Lobivia hertrichiana

Commonly used synonyms: *Lobivia (or Echinopsis) hertrichiana* is also known by a multitude of other names, including the quite frequently used *L. backebergii v. hertrichiana*.

Country of origin: Peru

It rapidly forms its low-growing clumps of many heads, which can readily be divided for propagation purposes. It is a variable species with reddish flowers. Although not the largest of flowers, the colour is often quite stunning. Some forms have flowers with a paler throat.

Lobivia maximiliana v. westii

Commonly used synonyms: Another plant with several names, this one is most commonly known as *Lobivia westii* or *Echinopsis maximiliana*.

Country of origin: Bolivia

There are several varieties of *L. maximiliana* and most are worth growing. Although it has smaller flowers than most lobivias, the flowers of *L. maximiliana v. westii* are very attractive, with an interesting shape and often with an almost metallic sheen to the petals.

cactus directory

Lobivia pentlandii

Commonly used synonyms: *Lobivia (or Echinopsis) pentlandii* is a variable species, consequently it is another plant with lots of names – many local variants have been separately named in the past.

Country of origin: Bolivia & Peru

It has stronger but more open spination than some of the smaller lobivias mentioned previously (*L. arachnacantha*, for example) and can have red, pink, orange or yellow flowers.

the cacti handbook

Lobivia tiegeliana

Commonly used synonyms: *Lobivia peclardiana, Echinopsis tiegeliana.*

Country of origin: Argentina & Bolivia

Lobivia tiegeliana is yet another example of a compact-growing lobivia with neat spination and beautiful flowers. Like so many lobivias, its variability has resulted in a number of varieties being named.

The lobivias shown barely scratch the surface of the huge number of species available. They do, however, illustrate the beauty of this easy-to-grow genus.

cactus directory

Lophophora williamsii

Country of origin: Mexico & southern USA

Known by the common name 'Peyote', *L. williamsii's* greatest claim to fame is that it is harvested from habitat for the hallucinogenic properties of the alkaloid mescaline that it contains. Sadly, this also leads to the theft of cultivated specimens. It is particularly unfortunate because tests have shown that the alkaloid is not present in cultivation – indeed consumption of these stolen specimens is likely to be harmful due to the application of insecticides or other chemicals.

These soft-bodied plants, with their large taproots, can be prone to splitting if their watering regime is increased too rapidly.

the cacti handbook

Mammillaria species

Country of origin: Caribbean, Central America, northern South America & southern USA

Even taking a conservative view, there are around 200 mammillaria species. Over the years there have probably been about three times that number of names in use.

Although a few are fiendishly difficult to grow, the huge majority present no difficulty whatsoever in cultivation and so are hugely popular among collectors. Indeed many growers specialise in mammillaria species to the exclusion of almost everything else.

With so many species, over such a wide range, it is inevitable that there will be a wide range of appearances and features. However, most mammillaria species tend to be low-growing, clumping plants, producing rings of fairly small pink or cream flowers on each of the plant's heads.

The species shown are merely a tiny sample, intended to show typical forms and features within the genus.

Mammillaria bocasana

Country of origin: Mexico

Mammillaria bocasana is often one of the first plants acquired by new growers. It is easy to grow and will clump rapidly if 'potted-on' regularly. It is occasionally pink flowered, but more usually it produces cream flowers – and plenty of them.

The pale spinination is attractive and looks soft, but be warned, this plant has 'fish-hooked' central spines, which easily attach themselves to skin or clothing. Handle the plant with care or you may damage it while seeking to free yourself from its spines.

Mammillaria duwei

Commonly used synonyms: *Mammillaria nana ssp. duwei, Mammillaria crinata ssp. duwei.*

Country of origin: Mexico

Mammillaria duwei is one of the more recent mammillaria species to be discovered and described, but it is quite readily available in cultivation.

It is usually solitary in habitat and even in cultivation it will often form a reasonable-sized head before it begins to offset. Its flowers are attractive, but to really appreciate the beauty of this plant – particularly the stronger-spined forms – you need to look at it very closely, preferably with a magnifying glass. Such examination will show that the spines appear to be covered with a coating of white frost.

cactus directory

Mammillaria elongata

Country of origin: Mexico

Mammillaria elongata is another plant that is often seen in collections. It is very variable in appearance and so it, and its subspecies *M. echinaria*, has accumulated a large number of dubiously named varieties.

The plant shown is the cristate form, which is often referred to as the 'Brain Cactus' because of its convoluted appearance. The normal form comprises a clump of large numbers of elongated stems each 1–3 cm (1/2–11/4 in) in diameter. The spination can range from yellow, through gold and brown, to a strong red. Although common, if several well-grown plants of different forms are displayed side-by-side the effect can be most impressive.

Mammillaria glassii

Country of origin: Mexico

Similar to *Mammillaria bocasana*, *M. glassii* quickly forms low-growing mounds of pale-spined heads. Its pale pink flowers are much smaller and, though pretty if examined closely, could not be described as eye-catching. The subsequently produced, maroon seedpods are much more noticeable.

The subspecies, *M. glassii ssp. Ascensionis*, has larger stems and considerably larger flowers.

Although a position in full sun is recommended in cultivation, if grown in hotter climates the provision of shade is advisable.

cactus directory

Mammillaria guelzowiana

Commonly used synonyms: *Krainzia guelzowiana.*

Country of origin: Mexico

Mammillaria guelzowiana has the white radial spines, hooked central spines and clumping habit of many other soft-bodied mammillaria species, but its brightly coloured flowers are huge by comparison.

Initially solitary, once *M. guelzowiana* clumps each head produces a ring of flowers and it is truly spectacular. There is a price to pay – it is harder to grow than most of its relatives. Free-draining compost and care with watering are essential.

There are a number of larger-flowered mammillaria species but they all seem to be considerably more susceptible to loss than many of the smaller-flowered ones. *Mammillaria (Krainzia) longiflora* and *M. saboae* are just a couple of them.

Mammillaria longimamma

Commonly used synonyms: *Dolicothele longimamma.*

Country of origin: Mexico

Mammillaria longimamma is very distinctive in appearance. It has extremely long tubercles and weak spinration, resulting in an appearance that is not favoured by everyone. It is, however, sufficiently different to add variety to a collection of otherwise similar-looking mammillaria species. Its best feature is the large, lemon-yellow flowers.

A deep pot will be needed as its tuberous root develops. Because of the consequential increase in the volume of compost, care should be taken to ensure that the plant is not over-watered.

Mammillaria perbella v. lanata

Commonly used synonyms: The correct name for this slow-growing plant is unresolved; opinion is divided between *Mammillaria perbella* and *M. pseudoperbella*.

Country of origin: Mexico

Whatever its correct name, it is included to illustrate the growth form of some *Mammillaria* species. It is neither solitary, nor does it produce offsets. Instead, when it matures, the growing point divides into two. Eventually, each new growing point will divide again to give a four-headed plant, and so on. The stems of *M. perbella* remain short, resulting in a low-growing, multi-headed plant. In some species, the plant grows taller but divides in the same way.

Mammillaria plumosa

Country of origin: Mexico

Mammillaria plumosa forms beautiful mounds of feathery, white heads. It comes in various forms, but the most attractive looks like a heap of soft golf balls. It has no central spines and the radials are so turned back and flexible that it is probably the most harmless of all cacti.

It can be reluctant to flower in cultivation, due to insufficient sunlight. Even when flowers do appear – often very late in the season – they are fairly insignificant, being pale and small.

M. carmenae is another similar, good-looking and safe-to-handle plant. Its heads are less globular and its straighter spines are more yellow than white.

cactus directory

Mammillaria senilis

Commonly used synonyms: *Mamillopsis senilis.*

Country of origin: Mexico

Mammillaria senilis has caused many debates among growers. Its large, red flowers, often dusted with yellow pollen, contrast beautifully with the brilliant white spination, but not everyone can persuade it to flower. For many years it was suspected that there were flowering and non-flowering forms in cultivation, but it is more likely that plants which would not flower were simply not getting sufficient sunlight.

In time the plant will form a large clump. A white-flowered form is seen occasionally.

Mammillaria surculosa

Commonly used synonyms: *Dolicothele surculosa.*

Country of origin: Mexico

Mammillaria surculosa used to be part of the old genus dolicothele. It is a much smaller growing than *M. longimamma* and forms a dense mat of small heads, just above the surface of the compost. Its bright yellow flowers are large for the size of the plant, plentiful and strongly citrus scented.

M. surculosa develops an extensive tuberous root and so care is required with watering and pot size selection.

cactus directory

Mammillaria zeilmanniana

Commonly used synonyms: Although some believe it to be a subspecies of *Mammillaria crinita*, this plant is almost invariably labelled *M. zeilmanniana*.

Country of origin: Mexico

Mammillaria zeilmanniana is so attractive when each of its hook-spined heads sports a crown of flowers that it has been mass-cultivated for the nursery trade. It is easy to grow and extremely rewarding with its flower production.

A splendid cristate form is frequently offered for sale, as is the slightly less often seen white-flowered form.

Matucana oreodoxa

Commonly used synonyms: *Borzicactus oreodoxus*.

Country of origin: Peru

Matucana (including submatucana) species are not seen for sale as often as they deserve to be. These hummingbird-pollinated plants produce their long, yellow, red, orange or pink flowers when they are still quite small.

Matucana flowers tend to be similar in shape and size (though some don't open as wide as others), but their bodies vary considerably, as indicated by three examples.

Matucana oreodoxa has a rounded, open-spined body and tends to remain solitary, although it may produce offsets with age.
M. madisoniorum has fewer spines, which have a tendency to fall off, leaving an almost completely bare body.

Matucana paucicostata

Commonly used synonyms: There are many names in use for this plant, the most frequent being: *Submatucana paucicostata, Borzicactus paucicostatus, Matucana senilis.*

Country of origin: Peru

Matucana paucicostata is an open-spined plant, but it is much less rounded in shape than *M. oreodoxa* and it clusters prolifically. It flowers freely and before long its offsets also flower, making it a splendid sight.

Although they enjoy a sunny position and can tolerate low temperatures, most matucana species are happy with partial shade – useful to know when positions in full sun are in short supply. A little extra heat in winter ensures that they do not mark from the cold.

Matucana weberbaueri v. flammeus

Commonly used synonyms: *Borzicactus weberbaueri*

Country of origin: Peru

The third body form of the matucana species is more densely covered with spines. Examples include *M. weberbaueri* and the more frequently seen *M. haynei*. The latter can be found under about 20 different names, indicating its variability.

The plant shown is the orange-flowered variety (*v. flammeus*). The type species *M. weberbaueri* has lemon-yellow flowers.

Melocactus matanzanus

Country of origin: Cuba

Melocacti look much like any other solitary, globular cacti when young, but once they reach maturity they develop their distinctive cephalium. When the cephalium begins to form the plant body growth is much reduced. Flowers and seedpods form from the cephalium, which becomes taller with each season's growth. *M. matanzanus* will begin to form its cephalium when the plant is still quite small, maybe as little as 8 cm (3 in) in diameter.

Melocacti are very sensitive to temperature and must be kept warm at all times.

Neoporteria gerocephala

Commonly used synonyms: *Neoporteria gerocephala* may be labelled as *N. nidus v. gerocephala* or, more recently, *Eriosyce senilis*. Indeed all the plants formerly assigned to the genera horridocactus, islaya, neochilenia, neoporteria, pyrrhocactus and thelocephala – and a few others besides – are now considered to be eriosyce species.

Country of origin: Chile

The extremely eye-catching, interwoven spination of this plant almost completely covers the body. How the bi-coloured flowers push through these spines undamaged is quite remarkable, but they do and they too are very attractive.

Other related species – or if you prefer varieties – such as *N. multicolor* and *N. senilis* are equally worth growing.

cactus directory

Neoporteria microsperma

Commonly used synonyms: *Neoporteria subgibbosa v. microsperma, Eriosyce subgibbosa.*

Country of origin: Chile

Although the flowers are similar to *Neoporteria gerocephala*, the spination is different. It is darker, stouter and much more open, allowing the dark body to show through. Initially globular, eventually the plant will elongate and become short columnar in form.

Although they need plenty of sunlight, care should be taken to avoid scorching neoporteria species, either by the provision of light shading in mid-summer or by good ventilation.

Neoporteria napina

Commonly used synonyms: Although now considered to be *Eriosyce napina*, this plant will often be labelled *Neoporteria napina*, or more likely by its even older name of *Neochilenia napina*.

Country of origin: Chile

This plant – and the other old *neochilenia* species – has funnel-form flowers, compared with the less open flowers of the typical neoporteria species.

N. napina is slow growing and tuberous rooted, thus requiring a deep pot and careful watering. Its grey-brown body seems to enhance its aged appearance, but it flowers readily enough.

Notocactus species

Country of origin: Argentina, Bolivia, Brazil, Paraguay & Uruguay

Despite the resistance of many growers, current thinking is that all notocactus species should be incorporated into the genus parodia. It will be a long time before growers and nurserymen rename all their plants – assuming they ever do – and so the name notocactus has been retained here.

Notocactus is another genus which is often favoured by beginners – and rightly so. They are generally readily available, easy to grow and free flowering.

Most species are happy if given partial shading, though a few of the non-clumping species will tend to grow over-tall with age, particularly in poor light, and will need to be replaced.

the cacti handbook

Notocactus haselbergii

Commonly used synonyms: *Brasilicactus haselbergii, Parodia haselbergii.*

Country of origin: Brazil

Notocactus haselbergii is one of two species formerly known as brasilicactus. *N. haselbergii* is the larger-growing species, with white spines and red flowers. *N. graessnerii* has golden spines and greenish flowers.

Both these species adopt an unusual growth habit. The growing point starts in the centre of the top of young plants, but it gradually moves down the side facing the sun, making the plant look as though it should be turned around to even up its growth. Most growers believe this is not the case and prefer to leave the plant to develop in a distinctive and strongly one-sided manner.

cactus directory

Notocactus leninghausii

Commonly used synonyms: *Eriocactus leninghausii, Parodia leninghausii.*

Country of origin: Brazil

Notocactus leninghausii will remain solitary for a number of years, even after it starts to produce its shiny, yellow flowers. Eventually its yellow-spined stem will begin to offset and, in time, if grown well, it will produce a magnificent clump with each stem flowering freely.

Most growers advocate partial shade for this plant, but some magnificent specimens have been grown in full sun without any detrimental effects.

Notocactus magnificus

Commonly used synonyms: *Eriocactus magnificus, Parodia magnifica.*

Country of origin: Brazil

Probably the most impressive of the notocactus species is the well-named *N. magnificus*. Its yellow spines grow neatly along its clearly defined ribs and contrast beautifully with the plant's blue-green body. With age it forms a splendid clump and freely produces its yellow flowers.

A little extra heat, or at least good air movement, should be provided in winter to avoid the risk of the body becoming marked.

cactus directory

Notocactus mammulosus

Commonly used synonyms: Many plants previously given their own names have been deemed to be synonyms of *Notocactus mammulosus*. However the most common are *Notocactus submammulosus* and *Parodia mammulosa*.

Country of origin: Argentina & Uruguay

Notocactus mammulosus is typical of many of notocactus species, in that it produces large, showy, silky, yellow flowers with a purple stigma. It is easy to grow and is strongly recommended to newcomers to the hobby, who want to see impressive flowers at an early age.

These plants sometimes suffer from 'corking' around the base. This is perfectly normal, if unsightly. It can be minimised by using an acid compost and a small amount of water on sunny days during the winter months to keep them growing.

Notocactus uebelmannianus

Commonly used synonyms: Parodia werneri.

Country of origin: Brazil

Apart from those species formerly known as brasilicactus, most notocactus have yellow flowers. The few species with other coloured flowers are keenly sought after – and not so often seen offered for sale. One such is the purple-flowered form of *N. uebelmannianus*. (There is also a yellow-flowered form, which is impossible to tell apart from the purple one until it flowers.)

Others with non-yellow flowers include *N. herteri*, *N. roseiflorus*, *N. roseoluteus* and *N. rutilans*, which all have pink or pink and yellow flowers.

cactus directory

Opuntia basilaris

Country of origin: Mexico & southern USA

There are many *Opuntia* species, but few can be recommended for cultivation. This is a shame because when seen as huge plants in habitat, or planted out in gardens – several species are winter hardy, even in cold climates – they make a splendid sight, with literally hundreds of beautiful flowers. Sadly, most species grow too large for the majority of growers and they do not flower readily with restricted root room.

Opuntia basilaris is commonly known as the 'Beavertail Cactus' because of the shape of its purple-tinted, blue-green pads. The plant shown is in habitat in Arizona, where it makes a wonderful sight when in bloom.

the cacti handbook

Opuntia microdasys

Country of origin: Mexico

Many opuntia species look – and indeed are – quite ferocious, their vicious armament making them rather dangerous for growing indoors. *O. microdasys* is without spines but, although it looks soft and harmless, it must still be treated with respect. The opuntia species without central spines have tiny glochids – small, loose spines that attach themselves to skin or clothing if touched. These glochids can cause skin irritation for several hours.

There are several, very attractive varieties of *O. microdasys* with white, brown, reddish or yellowish glochids. All stay quite small and so provide a means of growing a representative of the flat-padded opuntia species in cultivation.

cactus directory

Opuntia tunicate

Commonly used synonyms: Cylindropuntia tunicata.

Country of origin: Mexico

In addition to the flat-padded opuntia, there are branching, stem-like species called 'Chollas' in North America. The majority of these are too large for most collections, but there are a few smaller-growing species like *Opuntia tunicata*. The golden-spined form – *O. tunicata v. aureispina* is pictured. It will occasionally flower in cultivation.

It must be treated with great care, as the fierce-looking spines are both sheathed and barbed and are extremely painful to extract. Should a spine become embedded in the skin, first cut the spine from the plant and only then attempt to extract it.

Opuntia vestita

Commonly used synonyms: Austrocylindropuntia vestita.

Country of origin: Bolivia

Opuntia vestita grows into a branching plant covered with white hairs. Small leaves are initially present on young stems but they eventually die off when the stems grow longer. Although not readily visible because of the hairs, sharp glochids are present beneath them.

The plant shown is a cristate form. It needs regular maintenance to keep it looking cristate, as normal branches frequently sprout. If the branches were left in place the plant would eventually revert to its normal form.

cactus directory

Oreocereus trollii

Country of origin: Argentina & Bolivia

The various oreocereus species, although reluctant to flower in cultivation, serve to add variety of appearance to a mixed cactus collection. Many people find the white, woolly hairs covering the stems quite appealing.

As the plants get older, it is quite normal for the hairs towards the base of the plants to darken. Care should still be taken to keep them as clean as possible to avoid unsightly marks caused by dirt or mould developing if, for example, sticky nectar from another plant has dripped onto them.

Parodia species

Country of origin: Argentina & Bolivia

For growers who are short of space but want flowers, the inclusion of a few parodia species would be well worthwhile. The six plants shown would all fit into a space about 30 x 20 cm (12 x 8 in), yet they will each produce red, yellow or orange flowers on and off throughout the summer months.

The floral remains should be carefully removed after flowering. If they are left in position they may inhibit the next crop of flowers, although it is surprising how the new buds can push through them. If they are removed too soon or if too much force is used, spine clusters will be pulled off the plant, spoiling its appearance.

cactus directory

Parodia sanguiniflora

Commonly used synonyms: *Parodia sanguiniflora* (sometimes called *P. mutabilis v. sanguiniflora*) may, as some suggest, merely be one of many forms of *P. microsperma*.

Country of origin: Argentina

Parodia species are not often seen offered for sale, except from specialist sources. *P. sanguiniflora* freely produces its relatively large, red flowers, but almost any species would be worthy of consideration. Many remain solitary, but a few – such as the lovely orange-flowered *P. mairanana* – will clump freely.

Parodia sucrensis

Commonly used synonyms: Parodia tuberculata.

Country of origin: Bolivia

Parodia sucrensis is another solitary plant that can only be reproduced from seed. It has slightly smaller orange flowers than *P. sanguiniflora*, but there are plenty of them and they contrast nicely with the green body and white wool.

One or two parodia species – such as *P. schwebsiana* – produce copious quantities of this wool and are well worth seeking out.

cactus directory

Rebutia albiflora

Commonly used synonyms: **Aylostera albiflora.**

Country of origin: Bolivia

If just a single genus is to be recommended to a beginner, then rebutia must be the one. Although they are all low-growing, clumping plants, including species formerly known as aylostera, mediolobivia and digitorebutia, their range of flower colours and body forms is wide enough to make a collection of these alone. There have been attempts to incorporate sulcorebutia and weingartia within rebutia, but these suggestions have not proved popular with growers.

Rebutia albiflora quickly spreads to form clumps of small, pale-green stems, with very soft spines. It is named after its extremely prolific white flowers, although in reality the flowers usually have a hint of pink. The soft-bodied stems can be prone to scorching, so unless good air movement can be guaranteed some light shading is advisable.

Rebutia gibbulosa

Country of origin: Bolivia

Rebutia gibbulosa is a fairly recent introduction by Karel Knize under his field number KK 1563. It is typical of a good number of rebutia (or aylostera) species, with its globular, clustering body, tidy spinaton and numerous red flowers.

Rebutia species are generally easy to raise from seed and can flower after as little as 18 months, although two years is more usual. With few exceptions, they are also extremely easy to grow, provided their high-altitude origins are taken into account and they are given good light and cold winters. As long as they are completely dry, they should be untroubled by temperatures dropping below freezing point.

cactus directory

Rebutia heliosa

Country of origin: Bolivia

Although most rebutia species present no difficulties in cultivation, *R. heliosa* is one of the few exceptions. It well worth the effort, however, as its small heads with their tight, silvery spination make it a beautiful plant, even without its impressive orange flowers. It is reported to be usually solitary in habitat, but it inevitably forms clumps in cultivation.

A splendid hybrid between *R. heliosa* and *R. albiflora* has been widely circulated. This retains the typical 'mound' form of R. albiflora, but has more spines, silvery in colour, and freely produces apricot-coloured flowers.

Rebutia hoffmannii

Commonly used synonyms: It has been proposed that *Rebutia* (or *Aylostera*) *hoffmanii* is just a form of *R. spinosissima*. However, it will be a long time before the new name replaces its familiar one.

Country of origin: Argentina

This plant cannot be recommended highly enough. It has soft yellowish-white spination that, as well as being attractive, is unlikely to inflict pain on the unwary grower! Add to that its ease of cultivation – just give plenty of sunshine – and its ability to produce masses of orange flowers. As the plant becomes larger, so the number of flowers increases, virtually hiding the whole plant during its annual flowering peak. Most years it will obligingly produce a respectable second flush of flowers a few weeks later.

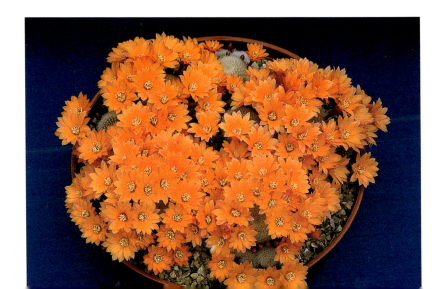

cactus directory

Rebutia marsoneri

Country of origin: Argentina

Rebutia marsoneri (sometimes considered a synonym of *R. krainziana*) is a welcome addition to a collection of rebutia species. Its bright-yellow flowers complement the more common reds, pinks and oranges.

When confronted by a dazzling array of colour from a collection of cacti such as these in full bloom, it is hard to understand why some nurserymen insist on spoiling cacti by gluing or pinning artificial blooms onto them. The fake flowers may last longer, but are nothing like as beautiful as the genuine ones and should be avoided.

Rebutia minuscula

Country of origin: Argentina

There are many forms or varieties of Rebutia minuscula. Most notable are *R. minuscula v. grandiflora* (similar but with larger, longer, tubed flowers) and *R. minuscula v. violaciflora*. Because of the number of forms in circulation, and the prolific seed setting of most rebutia species, resulting in many hybrids, it is not easy to be sure whether or not your plant is actually true to type.

Some experienced growers treat this widely distributed, easy-to-grow plant with some contempt, replacing it with smaller, more challenging plants. Those who continue to grow it, appreciate it for what its good at – flower power!

cactus directory

Rebutia minuscula v. violaciflora

Commonly used synonyms: *Rebutia violaciflora.*

Country of origin: Argentina

Rebutia minuscula v. violaciflora is well known for its shocking pink flowers. Smaller flowered than *R. minuscula*, what it loses in size, it more than makes up for with the eye-catching intensity of their colour.

As with all rebutia species, keep a wary eye open for attacks by red spider mites. These microscopic pests favour soft-bodied cacti and can quickly cause unsightly scarring at the growing points.

Rebutia muscula

Commonly used synonyms: *Aylostera muscula*.

Country of origin: Bolivia

Rebutia muscula is a worthy plant, even when it is not in flower. Its dense, white spines are attractive and soft to the touch. When it flowers, its clear, orange flowers contrast beautifully with the body of the plant.

Again it is easy to grow, but care must be taken to give it sufficient sun to prevent its soft stems becoming too long and too soft. Overhead watering should be avoided to keep its spination clean and dry.

cactus directory

Rebutia narvaecensis

Commonly used synonyms: For many years this plant was circulated under the name *Rebutia espinosae* and it is still often seen labelled either that or *Aylostera narvaecensis*.

Country of origin: Bolivia

The shocking pink of *R. minuscula v. violaciflora's* flowers is not to everyone's taste, but few could fail to appreciate the delicate colouring of the pink and white flowers of R. narvaecensis. The subtle colours make this one of the most beautiful of all cacti in flower – even when compared with the showy, larger-flowering plants.

Unusually for a *rebutia species*, *R. narvaecensis* does not readily produce seed.

Rebutia pygmaea v. haagei

Commonly used synonyms: *Mediolobivia haagei, Rebutia haagei*

Country of origin: Argentina

Rebutia pygmaea v. haagei is part of a variable group of plants that have been given many names. One major author recently listed it as having 64 synonyms. This combination of the entire mediolobivia sub-genus into the single species *R. pygmaea* may be scientifically valid, but such 'lumping' does not help when purchasing a specific form. Whatever the taxonomy, these plants are certainly worth growing.

They have slightly conical, short, columnar heads, often dark or greyish-green, sometimes bronze, brown or purplish in colour. The flowers of *R. pygmaea v. haagei* are usually salmon-pink, but like plants of the Mediolobivia subgenus they can have attractive two-tone petals.

cactus directory

Rhipsalidopsis gaertneri

Country of origin: Brazil

Rhipsalidopsis gaertneri is often called the Easter Cactus because in many countries its flowering season generally coincides with that time of year.

It is a Brazilian rainforest plant that grows as an epiphyte. Consequently, it requires different treatment from the majority of cacti. It needs warmth, shade, regular watering and fertiliser, which is perhaps why this plant is so often seen growing successfully as a houseplant.

It will flower prolifically, but once the buds begin to form it must be kept in the same orientation to the light – plants that are turned are prone to dropping their buds.

Rhipsalidopsis rosea

Commonly used synonyms: Both *Rhipsalidopsis rosea* species are sometimes referred to under other generic names including rhipsalis and hatiora.

Country of origin: Brazil

This plant is similar to *R. gaertneri* except that it has pink flowers, which, like the leaves, are significantly smaller. It is not seen as often as its larger relative, and has an annoying habit of collapsing, just when it seems to be growing well. Quite why it does this is unclear; some people can grow it without difficulty, yet others cannot. Both too much and too little water seem to cause problems. Growing it in an orchid mixture has proved successful for some growers.

cactus directory

Schlumbergera x buckleyi

Country of origin: Brazil

Strictly speaking it is incorrect to say that this plant comes from Brazil, as its hybrid origin is obviously nursery cultivated. However, with the exception of the somewhat distinctive – and difficult to grow – *S. opuntiodes*, it is virtually impossible to be sure that you have a true species rather than a hybrid. Two species, *S. bridgesii* and *S. truncata*, provide the main parentage of most hybrids. The latter, also known as *Zygocactus truncates*, is distinguished by its more upright habit and the pronounced toothed edges to its leaves. This plant is commonly known in many countries as the Christmas Cactus. Apart from a tendency to flower a month or two earlier than *Rhipsalidopsis gaertneri*, its main distinguishing feature is the flower shape, which is zygomorphic (that is, it is not fully symmetrical).

Schlumbergera hybrids

Country of origin: Nursery cultivated

There has been much hybridisation of schlumbergera plants and, as a result, a huge number of named and unnamed cultivars are in cultivation. Although growth habit and leaf size and shape can vary a little, the real difference is in the colour of the flowers. These can range from red, through various shades of pink, to the highly sought-after pure white. There is also a yellow-flowered cultivar, although this has a tendency to revert to pale-pink flowers if it is not kept warm enough.

As with all epiphytic cacti occasional spraying is advantageous. They must not be turned once the buds have formed, as this may cause the flowers to abort.

cactus directory

Setiechinopsis mirabilis

Commonly used synonyms: *Arthrocereus mirabilis, Echinopsis mirabilis.*

Country of origin: Argentina

Setiechinopsis mirabilis is a small plant that will never outgrow the space available. It will flower when its brownish body is only 8–10 cm (3–4 in) tall. The flowers are rather beautiful and very strongly perfumed – a strange scent, often likened to a type of ointment – but sadly they open in the evening and die by the following morning.

S. mirabilis is often considered to be short lived, growing from seed to maturity in just a few years, then dying for no obvious reason after a few flowering seasons. Extra winter warmth may help prolong its life, but it germinates freely from seed and it is likely that this early demise is normal.

Stenocactus species

Country of origin: Mexico

Often seen with the generic name of echinofossulocactus, the various stenocactus species are best known for their pronounced wavy ribs. The variability of these plants and the number of hybrids in cultivation make positive naming difficult.

They are not difficult to grow and their attractive ribs – more visible on the weaker-spined forms – make them worthy of inclusion in any collection. The flowers usually have a dark mid-stripe on a background of pink or cream.

cactus directory

Sulcorebutia arenacea

Country of origin: Bolivia

The Bolivian genus sulcorebutia contains many species that add greatly to cactus collections. They are generally easy to grow and quite hardy. Most remain a manageable size and readily produce their brightly coloured flowers.

S. arenacea is one of the more distinctive and easily recognisable species. Its globular shape and tight spiral spination is usually enough to enable recognition, even when its golden-yellow flowers are absent. It tends to remain solitary, its body growing steadily larger for a number of years, after which occasional offsets can be expected.

Sulcorebutia canigueralii

Country of origin: Bolivia

Sulcorebutia canigueralii and its various varieties are definitely worth searching for. It clumps readily and so can be easily propagated from offsets. Its relatively small heads are dark coloured, sometimes purplish-brown. Coupled with neat spinration, it makes a very tidy-growing plant. Its fiery bi-coloured red/yellow flowers ensure that it quickly catches the eye during the flowering season. A number of other, similar *Sulcorebutia* species – such as *S. verticillacantha* and its varieties – are equally worth growing.

The Andean origins of *Sulcorebutia* species mean they are all frost hardy, providing their compost is dry.

Sulcorebutia glomeriseta

Country of origin: Bolivia

There has been a move recently to return all the sulcorebutia species to the genus rebutia, from which they were separated a number of years ago. Most growers are resisting this trend because they believe 'sulcos' are sufficiently distinctive to be kept separate. *S. glomeriseta* is one of the species that straddle the two genera and shares characteristics of both.

Despite its flowers being rather small and a plain yellow – as opposed to the more vivid or bicoloured flowers of many sulcorebutias – it produces them in sufficient profusion to make up for any deficiencies.

the cacti handbook

Sulcorebutia menesesii

Country of origin: Bolivia

Sulcorebutia menesesii has fairly large heads for such a heavily clustering species. The plant shown was labelled *Sulcorebutia menesesii v. kamiensis* (field collection number LAU974). However, unlike the yellow-flowered species, that variety is supposed to have orange-red flowers.

For best results, sulcorebutia species, like rebutias and lobivias, should be given plenty of sunlight, acid compost and a cold, dry winter rest.

cactus directory

Sulcorebutia rauschii

Country of origin: Bolivia

S. rauschii is one of the very few sulcorebutia species that are more difficult to grow. As is usually the case with the harder species, it is worth the extra care needed.

Although it clumps at a very small size, there are few really large clumps around. Even so, it looks lovely when only 10 cm (4 in) or so across. A number of forms are in cultivation. Its short, cylindrical heads may be either a greyish-green or purplish colour and, in either case, its neat spination may be either black or golden. Its flowers are magenta.

Sulcorebutia steinbachii

Country of origin: Bolivia

Sulcorebutia steinbachii is a variable, low-growing, freely-clustering species often seen in cultivation. The variability of its spination and its flower colour – often red, but sometimes orange-red or magenta – has led to it being given many different names in the past. It has a tidy appearance and flowers well.

Like many – but not all – sulcorebutia, *S. steinbachii* has a tuberous taproot and must be given a deep enough pot to accommodate it.

The plant shown is the form often referred to as variety horrida (KK875). It has stronger spines and tends to be more columnar than the species.

cactus directory

Sulcorebutia tiraquensis

Country of origin: Bolivia

Considered by some taxonomists to be a form of *Sulcorebutia steinbachii*, *S. tiraquensis* and its varieties are very attractive plants. In particular, the larger-headed, less clustering forms, like the one shown, are quite different from the typical *S. steinbachii* and add variety to a collection of sulcorebutias.

Because of their neat appearance and vivid, freely produced flowers some growers choose to specialise their collections and grow only sulcorebutias, attempting to acquire as many different forms as they have space for. Such collections are useful for reference and stunning during the flowering season, but can lack the interest that comes from a variety of types of cactus.

Tephrocactus articulatus

Commonly used synonyms: *Opuntia articulata* (and variety *oligacantha*), *Opuntia papyracantha*, *Opuntia diademata*

Country of origin: Argentina

Tephrocactus species grow into spreading clumps of rounded stems. The stems are very lightly attached and the plants will frequently collapse into a heap of cuttings, particularly during their dormant season. A little water occasionally on sunny days in the winter may help to prevent the problem. Most are frost hardy but unless you are certain about the hardiness of a particular species, it is safer to keep them frost free. With its distinctive, long, papery spines, *T. articulatus* is one of the most notable of the tephrocactus species.

cactus directory

Thelocactus species

Country of origin: Mexico & southern USA

Most thelocactus species are fairly easy to grow, and even at a small size many will repay the grower by producing their relatively large flowers.

Perhaps the greatest problem that growers are likely to encounter is the formation of unsightly sooty mould. This will occur if the sugary solution exuded by the plants is not cleaned off during the growing season by occasionally spraying them with water.

Some taxonomists believe that some or all ancistrocactus, echinomastus, hamatocactus, glandulicactus and sclerocactus should be considered to be species of thelocactus. Others go further and include all of the above, including thelocactus, within ferocactus.

Thelocactus bicolor

Country of origin: Mexico & southern USA

Very widespread in habitat, and probably the most common thelocactus species in cultivation, is the Texan and Mexican plant, *T. bicolor*, along with its several varieties. It is a very variable species that has accrued many varietal names over the years. Most of its varieties are worth growing. The one shown is *T. bicolor v. bolaensis*, but the varieties *schwarzii* and *tricolor* are just as worthwhile.

cactus directory

Weingartia sucrensis

Commonly used synonyms: *Weingartia neocumingii v. sucrensis*

Country of origin: Bolivia

Weingartia is another genus that may or may not be validly named. It has been suggested that, for all their distinctive appearance, they should be considered as sulcorebutia species, or, as some botanists now believe, rebutia species. Nevertheless the name weingartia survives on plant labels. The species shown, *W. sucrensis*, is one of the more common.

Whatever the name, these smallish-growing, globular plants are a welcome addition to a collection. Most are free flowering, producing a ring of yellow or golden flowers around the crown of the plant each year. Although rarely seen, there are also one or two red flowered forms in cultivation.

other succulents

Other succulent plants

There are many more other succulents than there are cacti. However, experience shows that the majority of people who develop an interest in the 'other succulents' tend to grow mostly cacti first, and then start to specialise later. For this reason, there are disproportionately few 'other succulents'

ABOVE: Sanseveria gracilis – one of the more manageably sized members of the family. It produces short-lived, white flowers.

included in this book. The intention here is to 'wet your appetite', and if you become interested you can research them further.

As there are a huge number of other succulent species, and only limited space available, they have been listed by family group, instead of alphabetically by genera.

Agavaceae

Genera include: Agave, beschorneria, calibanus, cordiline, dasylirion, dracaena, nolina, sanseveria, yucca.

Distribution: Widespread throughout the drier tropical and sub-tropical regions of the world.

Although succulent enthusiasts grow members of the family Agavaceae, many species have only a limited degree of succulence. In agave and sanseveria species the leaves are succulent. However, in the case of some species, such as yucca and dracaena, it is the stems that store the moisture. Perhaps the most obviously succulent members of this family are the Mexican caudiciform species of nolina and calibanus.

Because of their size, many of the larger species of this family (the tree-like yucca and dracaena species and Agave americana, for example) are usually grown outdoors. Ideally, they are bedded out in warmer climates,

LEFT: Agave parryi starting to produce a flower spike in habitat in the Arizona mountains.

other succulents

where they can quickly grow into impressively big plants. Several of the larger more robust species of agave and yucca are very tough in cultivation and can be grown outdoors in quite cold conditions. However, they prefer some protection from extreme conditions, otherwise they will suffer and may become marked.

In general, it is the smaller-growing plants (such as Agave utahensis or A. victoriae-reginae and some sanseveria species), which amateur growers seek out and grow in their collections, mostly because they do not have the space available for the giant-growing species.

Although less threatening in appearance than many cacti, agave leaves can have toothed edges and each leaf has a strong terminal spine.

ABOVE: Agave flower spikes remain tall even when the plants have started to die.

the cacti handbook

This can be extremely painful if you become impaled on it – indeed many growers put a cork on the tip of any leaf that is in a position to cause injury.

Sometimes referred to as 'Century Plants' because of the long time they take to reach flowering size, when agave species do flower – which is considerably sooner than the

other succulents

hundred years implied by the common name – they are most impressive.

The larger ones produce inflorescences of up to 10 m (33 ft) in height.

However, these are terminal and the plant will die after flowering.

LEFT: Agave victoria-reginae – perhaps the agave with the tightest, neatest rosette of leaves.

BELOW: Yucca baccata – yucca plants take up a lot of space but the flowers are magnificent

Asclepiadaceae

Genera include: Brachystelma, caralluma, ceropegia, duvalia, echidnopsis, edithcolea, frerea, hoodia, hoya, huernia, orbea, piaranthus, pseudolithos, stapelia, tavaresia and trichocaulon, among others. Recent changes in taxonomy have seen the introduction of new genera and many species have been transferred from their previously well-known names.

Distribution: Although the majority of succulent species come from Africa, plants from this family can be found in many regions of the world.

Although succulent enthusiasts grow members of the family Agavaceae, many species have only a limited degree of succulence. In agave and sanseveria species the leaves are succulent. However, in the case of some species, such as yucca and dracaena, it is the stems that store the moisture. Perhaps the most obviously succulent members of this family are the Mexican caudiciform species of nolina and calibanus.

LEFT: Frerea indica – this trailing plant from India flowers regularly but needs to be kept warm and humid.

RIGHT: Huernia pillansii – most huernia species are not difficult to grow and are more likely to flower than some of the other genera in the family.

the cacti handbook

other succulents

Because of their size, many of the larger species of this family (the tree-like yucca and dracaena species and Agave americana, for example) are usually grown outdoors. Ideally, they are bedded out in warmer climates, where they can quickly grow into impressively big plants. Several of the larger more robust species of agave and yucca are very tough in cultivation and can be grown outdoors in quite cold conditions. However, they prefer some protection from extreme conditions, otherwise they will suffer and may become marked.

In general, it is the smaller-growing plants (such as Agave utahensis or A. victoriae-reginae and some sanseveria species), which amateur growers seek out and grow in their collections, mostly because they do not have the space available for the giant-growing species.

LEFT: Hoya pubicalyx – a close relative of the more often seen, white-flowered H. carnosa. If grown well it will produce scented flowers all year round.

the cacti handbook

Although less threatening in appearance than many cacti, agave leaves can have toothed edges and each leaf has a strong terminal spine. This can be extremely painful if you become impaled on it — indeed many growers put a cork on the tip of any leaf that is in a position to cause injury.

Sometimes referred to as 'Century Plants' because of the long time they take to reach flowering size, when agave species do flower — which is

other succulents

ABOVE: Ceropegia distincta – showing its unusual flowers.

LEFT: Stapelia grandiflora – its huge, hairy flowers are 10 cm (4 in) or more across.

considerably sooner than the hundred years implied by the common name – they are most impressive. The larger ones produce inflorescences of up to 10 m (33 ft) in height. However, these are terminal and the plant will die after flowering.

ABOVE: Hoya bella – a dainty hanging plant that freely produces waxy flowers.

LEFT: Orbea variegata – possibly the most common stapeliad in cultivation. Keep its flowers out of the sun to minimise the unpleasant odour.

BELOW: Orbea variegata – close examination of the flowers shows their complex structure

other succulents

Asphodelaceae

Genera include: Aloe, astroloba, gasteria and haworthia. This family used to be considered part of the Liliaceae (Lily family). Aloe species are sometimes considered to be part of a sub-family called Aloaceae.

Distribution: Africa, Madagascar and Arabia.

Most of these plants are grown for their appearance when not in flower. This is particularly true for haworthia species and those of the closely related genus astroloba. Although haworthia plants will readily produce flower spikes, they are long and thin with rather small, insignificant flowers. Some growers even go so far as to remove the flowers when they form, as they believe they

ABOVE: Gasteria armstrongii – a stemless South African plant with red flowers.

the cacti handbook

detract from the appearance of the plants. Aloe flowers are rather more impressive; indeed huge clumps can often be seen in botanical gardens in warm climates where these large plants in full bloom make an impressive sight. The most frequently seen aloe species are probably Aloe aristata, A. variegata and A. vera. The latter is well known for its medicinal qualities, but it tends to grow too large for many indoor collections. The smaller-growing species, which usually form clumps of fairly low-growing rosettes, are much better suited for indoor cultivation than the longer-leafed or taller-growing, more sprawling species. To prevent them from becoming pale and excessively tall, aloe species should be given bright light. In full sunshine some species will turn a reddish colour; this is perfectly natural and is not in any way harmful. Scorching must, of

other succulents

course, be avoided on plants grown under glass. The tall 'tree' aloes, such as A. pillansii, are obviously unsuitable for indoor cultivation.

Haworthia species are popular in collections; their clustering rosettes of leaves make them attractive to many growers. The range of leaf shapes and the patterns of the whitish markings and translucent 'windows' give plenty of opportunity for collectors to seek out the more interesting forms. Although sometimes thought unexciting by cactus growers or by those who seek showy blooms, a good collection of the more interesting haworthia species can be most impressive. Like the aloe species, haworthia plants will colour up and go reddish brown in sunlight. Some growers advocate growing them in bright light,

LEFT: Haworthia flowers are not showy, but some are quite pretty if examined through a magnifying glass.

RIGHT: Aloe haworthiodes – one of the choicer, miniature species of Aloe from Madagascar.

BELOW: Aloe species will flower in cultivation, although the larger ones tend to take up more space than many growers can spare.

other succulents

while others prefer to keep them in shadier places where their leaves will stay a rich, dark green. Although some haworthia species are very slow growing, and a few are quite difficult in cultivation, most are easy. As the harder-to-grow ones are less easy to propagate they are less often seen offered for sale, so generally speaking any available species that catches the eye is probably worth buying.

RIGHT: Aloe variegata - easy to grow and often dismissed as common by experienced growers, it is a striking plant.

BELOW: Haworthia emelyae v. sanikraal and H. retusa v. dekenahii starting to flower at quite a small size.

other succulents

201

FAR LEFT: Aloe variegata - easy to grow and often dismissed as common by experienced growers, it is a striking plant.

LEFT: Aloe aristata – although very difficult to kill, this plant needs good light and not too much water to keep it looking its best.

BELOW: showing different leaf shapes and patterns.

Crassulaceae

Genera include: Adromiscus, aichryson, aeonium, cotyledon, crassula, dudleya, echeveria, greenovia, kalanchoe, pachyphytum, sedum, sempervivum, tacitus and tylecodon.

Distribution: Widespread, throughout most parts of the world.

Third largest of the families containing exclusively succulent plants, the Crassulaceae includes a large number of mainly leafy succulents. The widespread distribution of this family means that different plants come from widely differing habitats – as diverse as the Namibian desert and the Arctic Circle. Therefore, they require widely differing cultivational conditions. Many are, however, extremely undemanding. Some – including some Alpine species of sedum and most

LEFT: Adromiscus cooperi – easily propagated from leaves, some adromiscus form interesting little plants, although their flowers are rather insignificant.

RIGHT: Echeveria leucotricha is a Mexican plant with grey, felted leaves with brown tips, very similar to the more frequently seen Kalanchoe tomentosa from Madagascar.

the cacti handbook

RIGHT: Crassula tecta v. klingsbergensis – a small-growing crassula with interesting round flower heads.

BELOW: Aeonium canariense – aeonium rosettes die off after flowering.

other succulents

sempervivum species – are completely hardy outdoors, even in temperatures well below freezing, providing they are grown in a well-drained location, such as a rock garden or a grit-filled trough. Others, such as some of the larger echeveria species, can be grown decoratively outdoors during the summer months, but must be dug up and brought back into shelter if there is a danger of frost.

Some of the most frequently grown species are the rosette-forming plants. These include aeonium, dudleya, echeveria, sempervivum and tacitus species. The wide range of leaf size and colour of the various echeveria

TOP RIGHT: Sempervivum species – most 'House Leeks' are hardy outdoors without protection in Britain, provided they are in a well-drained and sheltered location.

RIGHT: Sedum morganianum is easy to grow in a hanging basket, but care is needed when handling it, as its leaves are easily detached from the stems.

the cacti handbook

species and cultivars make this genus suitable for growers who want to specialise. To see these plants at their best, grow them in strong light to make them colour up. It is important to avoid high nitrogen feeds that would cause them to become weak and leggy. A number of species develop a beautiful blue, farinose coating on the leaves. These must not be handled as the coating will become marked and the appearance of the plant spoilt. Others (e.g. Echeveria leucotricha and Kalanchoe tomentosa) produce felted leaves.

BELOW: Kalanchoe cultivar – whereas the K. blossfeldiana hybrids have small upward-facing flowers, other Kalanchoe cultivars have bell-shaped flowers.

ABOVE: Crassula ovata is a frequently grown plant, which – contrary to popular opinion – will flower each year in winter if kept in a very cool place and given bright light.

The easy propagation of Crassula ovata (sometimes called C. argentea, C. portulacaceae, or erroneously C. arborescens, which has more glaucous leaves), and its ability to flourish in a wide variety of conditions, including positions with quite poor light, have made it one of the most frequently seen members of this family. Its succulent stems will grow into a tree shape, covered in thick, rounded succulent leaves. Old specimens may reach as much as 1.5 m (5 ft) or more in diameter if given the space and root room. Many growers fail to bring C. ovata into flower but, provided it is given a bright position and very cool winter temperatures, it should produce its pinkish-white, star-shaped flowers each winter.

In recent years, a number of species have become increasing popular in garden centres. In particular, Tacitus bellus, with its neat rosettes and bright-pink flowers, and cultivars of Kalanchoe blossfeldiana, with their small but brightly coloured flowers.

Despite their insignificant flowers, some growers find the various forms of adromiscus attractive. They do not take up a lot of space and the various species include a number with leaves of interesting shapes, colours and markings.

other succulents

LEFT: Echeveria setosa v. deminuta (often labelled E. rundellii) is one of the prettiest echeverias, with neat, blue rosettes and small but striking flowers.

BELOW: Crassula falcata is not particularly eye-catching, until it produces its stunning red flower heads.

the cacti handbook

other succulents

The flowers of genera such as aeonium, greenovia and sempervivum are good to look at, but sadly their appearance means that the rosette from which they grew is about to die. Fortunately, in most cases, it will have produced offsets and so, though the appearance of the plant may be spoiled, it should not be lost altogether. Propagation of most species is easiest by means of rooted cuttings. This may be of branches or offsets. In some instances, even single leaves will easily root and produce plantlets. In the case of some kalanchoe species (such as K. daigremontiana, formerly known as Bryophyllum daigremontiana), tiny, already rooted plantlets form around the perimeter of the leaves. These rapidly become established on contact with compost. For many growers the novelty soon wears off

ABOVE: Tacitus bellus is another Mexican plant whose neat rosettes and bold flowers have made it popular in the horticultural trade.

when they become too invasive. Beginners would be well advised to avoid tylecodon species, as these tend to be more difficult to grow. Some are also highly toxic.

BELOW: *Kalanchoe blossfeldiana* cultivar – these cultivars are becoming increasingly popular in garden centres. Their striking flowers may be yellow, orange, red or one of several shades of pink.

other succulents

Euphorbiaceae

Genera include: Euphorbia, jatropha, monadenium and pedilanthus.

Distribution: Many parts of the world, but most of the succulent species are found in Africa, Madagascar, Arabia and parts of Asia, with some from the Americas.

The Euphorbiaceae, or Spurge family, includes both succulent and non-succulent species. Many growers of succulents include at least a few species in their collections, while others specialise in growing members of this large family.

Species range in size from the tiny to huge branching clumps many metres across and/or of great height. Some of the choicest species are caudiciform, with just a few small stems or leaves showing above the soil; others are towering plants up to 12 m (40 ft) in height. Many species grow deciduous leaves, others are spiny and cactus-like, while yet others remain smooth skinned. It is probably this diversity that makes this family so attractive to growers.

Some of the more popular and frequently seen species include Euphorbia mammillaris, E. meloformis, E. milii (Crown of Thorns) and E. obesa. More experienced enthusiasts will seek the choicer and more difficult species, such as E. abdelkuri, E. decaryi, E. gymnocalycioides and E. piscidermis. The more challenging species tend to be those from Arabia, Ethiopia

PREVIOUS PAGE: Euphorbia obesa is a small plant from South Africa. Despite its tiny, insignificant flowers, it remains a firm favourite with succulent growers.

RIGHT: Euphorbia mammillaris v. minima is a small-growing, but freely branching species from South Africa.

other succulents

215

the cacti handbook

ABOVE: Euphorbia milii v. splendens – central in this bed of euphorbia species. The Crown of Thorns is one of the most commonly grown species.

RIGHT: Euphorbia canariensis – this huge plant growing in habitat on the island of Gran Canaria looks superficially like a cactus.

other succulents

and Madagascar, with many of the easier-to-grow species originating from South Africa.

Some, such as E. obesa, can be readily grown from seed. As these plants, like many euphorbia species, are either male or female, one of each is necessary for pollination to take place. Care must be taken once the round pods, each containing three seeds, begin to form. When ripe the seedpods explode and, if they are not contained, can throw the seeds a considerable distance.

the cacti handbook

Those species that form a caudex – like caudiciform plants from most families – are generally expensive to buy and easy to kill. For this reason, they are not usually considered suitable for beginners. Although in their natural habitat the caudex would grow beneath the soil with just the stems and/or leaves showing, it is customary for growers to lift them in the pot, displaying the caudex above the surface of the compost. Apart from the obvious fact that there is otherwise little to see, this helps keep the caudex dry and reduces the risk of it rotting.

LEFT: Jatropha berlandieri – most caudiciform plants are expensive and keenly sought after. They are not recommended for beginners because they are prone to loss due to rot.

RIGHT: A selection of smaller-growing Euphorbia species, showing their diversity of appearance.

Warning!

Always take care when handling euphorbia species. If they are damaged they will exude a whitish sap that, in many species, is highly toxic and/or a skin irritant. Never allow this sap to come into contact with the eyes, and always wash any splashes from the skin immediately. Particular care must be taken, and personal protection (e.g. goggles) worn, when taking cuttings from these plants. Always wash hands thoroughly immediately afterwards.

Mesembryanthemaceae

Genera include: Of the 120 or more genera in this family, probably the best known are aloinopsis, argyroderma, carpobrotus, cephalophyllum, chasmatophyllum, cheiridopsis, conophytum, delosperma, dinteranthus, drosanthemum, ebracteola, faucaria, fenestraria, frithia, gibbaeum, glottiphyllum, lampranthus, lithops, mesembryanthemum, nananthus, odontophorus, pleiospilos, ruschia, stomatium, titanopsis and trichodiadema.

Distribution: Most species are native to southern and south-western Africa, with others from Madagascar and Arabia. Mesembs also grow in many other parts of the world, although whether this is their natural habitat or whether humans introduced them there is uncertain.

LEFT: Conophytum uviforme is one of relatively few night-flowering Conophytum species. Its flowers are strongly scented.

RIGHT: Faucaria albidens – the toothed leaves of some faucaria species, particularly F. tigrina, sometimes give the erroneous impression of being fly-catchers.

other succulents

221

To be more correct, this family should be called the Aizoaceae. However, the succulent members of it are generally called Mesembryanthemaceae or by the more familiar term Mesembs. The Mesembryanthemaceae is another family that attracts specialist collectors, as well as managing to get a specimen or two into most general collections. Despite the many other genera, lithops, is probably

ABOVE: Drosanthemum hispidum – the plant shown is hardy, even in a poorly drained and shady position outdoors in the north-east of England.

RIGHT: Pleiospilos compactus ssp. minor – the petals of Pleiospilos flowers grow longer as the flower gets older. Several species have interestingly scented flowers.

other succulents

the first Mesemb to catch the attention of almost every grower. These plants are commonly known as 'Living Stones' because of their distinctive appearance; even the name lithops is derived from Greek words meaning 'stone-like'. Their leafless, low-growing habit means that Lithops are almost perfectly camouflaged among stones and pebbles in their natural habitat in South Africa, Namibia and Botswana. In cultivation, careful selection of a variety of those species with attractive coloration and patterning makes for a fascinating collection. Most will readily produce their yellow or white flowers in the autumn.

the cacti handbook

Somewhat similar in their appearance, though usually with smaller, more prolifically clustering heads, are the conophytum species. They include species that used to be considered part of a separate genus called opthalmophyllum. While a few grow quite large, the majority are miniatures, flowering when small, and capable of putting on a lovely show of pink, white, orange and yellow flowers late in the growing year, after most other plants have started to go into winter dormancy. A small number of them are night flowering and tend to be highly scented.

Other genera to look out for include faucaria (most have toothed leaves and yellow flowers), pleiospilos (very fragrant flowers), frithia (stemless, with distinctive grey, finger-like leaves, and lovely pink, white and yellow flowers) and titanopsis (attractive, warty leaves). Indeed most of the smaller-sized species are well worth growing.

RIGHT: Frithia pulcra is not the easiest plant to grow well; it has a distinctive appearance and beautiful flowers.

other succulents

the cacti handbook

other succulents

Many Mesembs are ideal for growing in outdoor beds in warm countries, where they quickly spread to produce dense mats of leaves covered in flowers. A few are even hardy in colder climates. Some species, such as Drosanthemum hispidum, may defy the requirement for a sheltered, well-drained location, and survive and flower even in the most unlikely locations. Others are often seen growing outdoors as half-hardy annuals. They include 'Livingstone Daisies' (Doreanthus bellidiformis, also sometimes known as D. criniflorum). Although their flowering season lasts only a few

LEFT: Conophytum species – these small-growing plants give a lovely show of colour when still small. The entire group shown takes up an area of only about 25 x 15 cm (10 x 6 in).

ABOVE: Lithops dorotheae – apart from their curiosity value, the variety of colours and patterns make collections of lithops interesting.

weeks, their spectacular show of vibrant colours when the summer sun is shining on them is a sight to behold.

Many Mesemb genera grow to a strict seasonal timetable. They have distinct growth, flowering and resting periods, which must be respected by the grower. As these vary with the seasons in different parts of the world, growers should find out the optimum growing seasons for specific plants in their own countries. As a rule-of-thumb, give the plants

other succulents

a small amount of water on warm days and see how they respond. If they ignore it, leave them alone, if they show signs of growth, give them a little more a few days later as they are probably entering in their growing season.

Lithops grow during summer and autumn; they should be left dormant during winter and early spring, only being watered again when the bodies from the previous season are dried out and papery. The new head (or heads – this is how the plant increases its number of heads) will then push out from within the old sheath. If it is watered too soon, the old heads will not dry out properly and the plant will become deformed and weakened.

Propagation of Mesembs may be from seed or, for many of the multiple-stemmed or multi-headed species, by means of vegetative cuttings. The very fine seeds form in distinctive capsules, which, when ripe, will open when they get wet. This technique has evolved to allow seeds to escape during rainfall, when the growing conditions will give them the best chance of germination.

ABOVE: Carpobrotus edulis is found on coastlines in many parts of the world. Carpobrotus spread readily and flower abundantly.

the cacti handbook

Other succulent families

The families described above are the principal ones that contain succulent plants, but there are others. The family Apocynaceae contains some well-known succulent genera, including adenium and pachypodium. Others include the Compositae (othonna and senecio or kleinia species), the Geraniaceae (sarcocaulon and some succulent pelargonium species), the Portulacaceae (anacampseros, avonia, some lewisia species and portulaca), the Vitaceae (the Virginia Creeper family, which includes some caudiciform species of cissus and cyphostemma). Even the cucumber family (Cucurbitaceae) includes a few succulent species.

Whereas all the members of the cactus family and the Crassulaceae are succulent, as are the majority of the Asclepiads and the Mesembs, in the case of most other plant families relatively few species have evolved with succulent characteristics. Also, as with any evolution process, there are grey areas

LEFT: Kleinia articulata is one of the succulent members of the Compositae family.

other succulents

LEFT: Lewisia brachycalyx is a member of the Portulacaceae family. Like many lewisia species it has a small caudex and so is considered by many to be a succulent.

where plants are borderline species. They may, for example, have slightly thickened leaves or stems, but it is a matter of opinion as to whether they qualify as a bona fide succulent or not. Does that matter? Not if the plant appeals to the grower. It should not be excluded merely because it may not be truly succulent.

RIGHT: Pachypodium lameri of the family Apocynaceae can reach 8 m (26 ft) tall in habitat in Madagascar. Even in cultivation they can easily reach 2 m (6.5 ft) in height.

Glossary

The following definitions are provided as an aid to understanding the technical terms in this book. Some of the meanings have been simplified.

Areole The oval-shaped places, often woolly, from where spines or spine remnants grow on a cactus. Commonly referred to as 'spine cushions'.

Binomial Two-part scientific name of a plant, comprising Latin genus and species names. If a third name is added to denote subspecies or variety, strictly it becomes a 'Trinomial'.

Botanist A scientist who studies plant life.

Cactus *(plural cacti.)* A member of the family Cactaceae.

Calcareous Alkaline, containing lime.

Caudex A much enlarged, tuberous part of the stem or root system.

glossary

233

Caudiciforme A species of plant that will form a caudex.

Cephalium A specialised growth, often bristly, from which flowers and seedpods develop.

Cereoid A tall-growing cactus, typically branching with 'arms'. The word is derived from the genus cereus.

Chlorophyll Chemical compound, green in colour, which allows a plant to photosynthesise (that is, convert carbon dioxide into carbohydrates under the influence of light).
Clumping A plant that throws multiple side shoots to form a group of heads from a common base or stem.

Columnar Forming a column – tall, relative to its diameter.

Cristate A crested form of a plant, where the growing tip (or more unusually the flower) has elongated, often into a convoluted shape.

the cacti handbook

Cultivation The tending of plants by people. 'In cultivation' refers specifically to the growing of plants in a manmade environment.

Deciduous A plant that sheds its leaves under certain climatic conditions, or at a particular time of the year.

Detritus Accumulated waste matter, particularly organic, such as fallen petals or leaves.

Epiphyte Plant that grows epiphytically, that is, without its roots in the soil. Often found on trees where roots grow on the bark or in pockets of leaf mould, etc.

Etiolate To grow tall and thin due to insufficient light.

Family A taxonomic classification grouping, comprising related genera.

Farinose Covered with a white, grey or bluish powdery coating.

glossary

Form *(or forma)* The lowest ranking taxonomic classification. Usually used to define local variation of appearance.

Genus *(plural genera.)* A taxonomic classification grouping comprising related species.

Glaucous Covered with a grey, blue or white bloom.
Globular Ball shaped.

Glochid Small, thin, loose spines, which are barbed and detach from the plant if touched.

Grafting The bonding of two dissimilar plants, usually a weak or slow-growing plant onto a vigorous rootstock, to aid survival, speed up growth and/or as a propagation aid.

Habitat The place where a plant grows naturally.

Humus Decaying organic matter, e.g. leaf mould, used as part of a mixture of compost.

Hybrid Cross between two plants of different species.

Inflorescence A modified branch forming a structure to carry flowers.

Lumping A term used to describe the inclusion of a large number of previously individually named forms of a plant under a single name. The opposite of this is 'splitting'.

Mesemb An abbreviated name for a member of the Mesembryanthemum family (Aizoaceae).

Monstrose A monstrous form of a plant. Often where, instead of the usual single growing point, multiple points have developed.

the cacti handbook

Nomenclature The system and rules for the naming of plants (and other living things).

Propagation The production of multiple plants from a single plant (typically by offsets or cuttings) or from a pair of plants (by means of seeds).

Solitary A plant that remains a single stem and does not clump.

Species The basic unit in the taxonomic classification system. Usually considered to comprise individuals that can interbreed and produce consistent offspring.

Stapeliad Member of the family Asclepiadaceae.

Subspecies A taxonomic classification grouping of lower rank than species. Usually used to define notable variation of characteristics of insufficient merit to warrant species status.

Succulent A plant that has evolved the capacity for water retention.

Synonym A different name sometimes used to refer to the same plant.

Taxonomist Someone who studies nomenclature.

glossary

Taxonomy The study of nomenclature.

Tubercle Outgrowth from the body of a cactus on which the areole is usually located.

Variety A taxonomic classification grouping of lower rank than species. Usually used to define notable variation of characteristics of insufficient merit to warrant species status. Similar to, but lower ranking than, subspecies.

Viability The ability of seeds to germinate – 10% viability would result in only one in ten seeds germinating.

Zygomorphic With only one plane of symmetry – applicable to the flowers of schlumbergera.

Index

A

acanthocalyciums	62
Agavaceae	184-187
Apoynaceae	230
aporocactus	63
aporophyllum hybrids	64
areoles	13
ariocarpus species	65
Asclepiadadeae	188-194
Asphodelaceae	195-201
astrophytums	66-69

B

binomials, Latin	17
borzicactus	70

C

Cactaceae (family)	12-13
cacti	
- cultivation	22-25
- definition of	12
- directory	57-181
- habitat	18-21
- increasing your collection	54
- problems	44-53
- propagation	36-43
cephalocereus	71
cereus group	72-73
chamaecereus	75
chamaelobivia hybrids	76
cleistocactus	77-78
Compositae	230
copiapoas	79-80
coryphanthas	81
compost	34
Crassulaceae	202-212
cuttings, growing from	41

D

diseases	50

E

echinocactus	82
echinocereus	83-89
echinopsis species	90-93
echinopsis hybrids	94
epiphyllums	95
epiphyllum hybrids	96
epithelantha	97
espostoas	98
escobarias	99-100
Euphorbiaceae	213-219

F

ferocactus	101-103
fertiliser	35
fraileas	104

G

index

Geraniaceae	230
glossary	232-237
grafts, growing from	43
gymnocalyciums	105-110

H
haageocereus species	111
hamatocactus	112

L
leuchtenbergias	113
light for growing	30
lobivias	114-120
lophophoras	121

M
mammillaria species	122-133
matucanas	134-136
melocactus	137
Mesembryanthermaceae	220-229

N
neoporterias	139-140
notocactus species	141-146

O
offsets, growing from	42
opuntias	147-150
oreocereus	151

P
pachypodiums	20
parodias	152-154
pests	45-49
Portulaceae	230

R
rebutias	20, 155-164
repotting	32-34
rhipsalidopsis	165-166

S
schlumbergias	167-168
seed raising	36-40
setiechinopsis	169
spine cushions, *see areoles*	
stenocactus	170
sulcorebutia	171-177

T
taxonomy	14-17
temperature for growing	28
tephrocactus	178
thelocactus	179-180

W
watering	26
weingartias	181
where to grow cacti and succulents	23-25

Bibliography

Anderson, E.F., The Cactus Family, published by Timber Press, 2001.
Benson, L., The Cacti of United States and Canada, published by Stanford, 1982.
Eggli, U., Glossary of Botanical Terms with Special Reference to Succulent Plants, published by BCSS, 1993.
Innes, C. & Glass, C., The Illustrated Encyclopaedia of Cacti, published by Headline (1991).
Pilbeam, J., Cacti for the Connoisseur, published by Batsford (1987).
Preston-Mafham, R. & K., Cacti – The Illustrated Dictionary, published by Blandford (1991).
Rowley, G., Name That Succulent, published by Stanley Thornes (Publishers) Ltd., 1980.
Smith, G.F. et al, Mesembs of the World, published by Briza Publications, 1998.
Stearn, W.T., Botanical Latin, published by David & Charles, 1966.
International Code of Botanical Nomenclature (Tokyo Code), published electronically on-line by The International Association for Plant Taxonomy.

Credits

Grateful thanks go to those who helped make this book possible:
The following growers who allowed pictures to be taken of their plants for inclusion in the book:

Viv Brooks, John Gamesby, Roger Goodswen, Doreen Rippon, Margaret Spencer
Betty & Brian Unwin, Jack Voase

Roger Goodswen and Graham Walker for proofreading and helping me to minimise the number of errors in this book.

Those members of the Teesside Branch of the BCSS who provided advice and encouragement when I was just beginning my collection – and who still do!

And not forgetting...
...Ann for putting up with the ever-increasing number of plants in and around the house and the amount of my time spent looking after them, and for proofreading the draft text of this book.